GIRLS LIKE ME

12 SHORT BIBLE STUDIES ABOUT BIBLICAL WOMEN

SHELBIE MAE

To all my small group girls.

INTRODUCTION

Dear Girl,

Have you ever wanted to read the Bible more but didn't know where to start? Have the passages seemed too heavy, confusing, or hard to read? I think we can all say "yes" to one of these questions.

The heart behind this book is *you*. Yes, *you*.

I've been in student ministry for over five years and have met girls who *want* to read the Bible but lack motivation. Some have attended church for years yet are unaware of the stories about the awesome women in the Bible. This book was created to help girls navigating high school, college, first jobs, boyfriends, new husbands, and new babies read the Bible more.

But not only *read* but *relate*.

When we think of the Bible it's hard to see reflections of ourselves in the characters we read about. How could we be like Eve, the mother of all humanity, Deborah the warrior, or Esther the queen? They lived *thousands* of years ago. The truth is, we have a lot in common with them. They are *girls like us*. They struggled with lies, sexual abuse, and inner turmoil. They were also redeemed, strong, and brave. If we read their stories, we can find many commonalities.

Girls Like Me is meant to help you read the Bible, but here's the deal: You still have to do the work. You are the girl who must pick up her Bible or find a version on her phone, or the internet, or a podcast, and read.

In your hands, you have twelve small studies ranging from 3 days to 14 days. These stories are not in chronological order. Take your time, this is not a yearly devotional. This is a resource to help you dig deeper into scripture, and in turn, learn more about God.

Each day is broken into four parts.

1. **Girl Read.** Some days you will read a few verses and others you will read a whole chapter. But never *more* than a chapter. The studies are meant to be easy and manageable. All the scriptures in this book are from the NIV Bible unless otherwise noted.

2. **Girl Life.** This is where I share a good, bad, scary, or personal story from *my* life to help you apply what you have read to *your* life. This is not meant to be a devotional where you simply read what's on the page. It is meant to be a companion to reading the noted scriptures.

3. **Girl Do.** This is where we get practical. Where you can discover how to apply what you read to your life, *right now*.

4. **Girl Ask.** The end of each day will leave you with a question to consider. You can journal it if you want or read and run.

At the end of each study, there is a letter written just for you. I have signed them, A Girl Who Cares. I hope you find encouragement in the letters.

Girls Like Me has been written for you. If you have a digital copy, highlight it. If you have a paperback, write in it. Let God speak to you through the stories of the women recorded here. God has special things to say to each of us. You can discover the hidden words meant for your heart when you pick up his love letter and read it for yourself.

Some of the stories you will read will seem strange, sad, angering, or surprising. God's word is filled with stories that teach us about who God is. I hope God speaks to you as you read and shows you things that I never could have thought of. That's the beauty of the Bible. God shows each of us different things. He knows our hearts and gives them gentle nudges when we read the pages. That is one of the beautiful things about Scripture and one of the reasons I hope this book encourages you to cultivate a daily Bible reading routine.

Love,

Shelbie

You can find out more about me at the end of this book.

A NOTE ON MARRIAGE AND WOMEN IN BIBLICAL TIMES

Many of the stories discussed in this book showcase families with multiple wives. If your first response is, "No thank you." Having more than one wife is *no bueno*." I'm right there with you. But it is important to know as you read these stories that having more than one wife was a common practice in the Old Testament (the first two thirds) of the Bible. With that in mind, it is also important to note that this was not how marriage was created.

Jesus quotes Genesis in Matthew 19:4-6:

"Haven't you read," he replied, "that at the beginning the Creator 'made them male and female', and said, 'For this reason a man will leave his father and mother and become one flesh? So they are no longer two, but one..."

In this instance, one plus one (or one man plus one woman), equals one. They are joined.

There are many forms of marriage in the following stories. Some men had multiple wives and mistresses. One girl and her sister were married to the same man. Another girl was used by a married man to produce children.

Women did not have the same rights they experience today. In Biblical times women were valued more for their ability to birth children than for their minds or hearts. In contrast, many women in Biblical times were loved and cherished for who they were as women. The Bible is filled with stories, history, and ultimately God's love. Genesis makes it clear that both man and woman were created in the image of God.

So God created man in his own image,

in the image of God he created him;

male and female he created them. Genesis 1:27

Girls and women are not less because they are female. We are all beautiful creations of God.

The Bible documents more stories of men than women, but it is important to know that God loves and sees women. For generations, God has shown his love for women, and the Bible details some of those stories.

I hope God speaks to you through the life of these women and draws your heart closer to him. We are not less because we were born women. We are awesome children of God who have important roles to play.

WHAT CHRISTIAN GIRLS BELIEVE AND WHY

Girls Like Me is founded on The Gospel which is Christian - talk to explain salvation. If the idea is confusing or strange let me try to break it down for you, girl-to-girl.

The breakdown:

We were each born into this world as a sweet innocent baby. We had cute chubby cheeks, rolls on our legs, and sparkly eyes. We may have been planned by our parents or they might admit we were a surprise. Regardless of our parents' wishes, we are a carefully thought-out piece of art created by God. But we were not his first amazing, unique, and beautiful creation.

Thousands of years ago God made Adam and Eve and placed them in a perfect utopia. He made them in his image to take care of the world. God was so close to Adam and Eve that he walked alongside them, in relationship with them. The keyword here is the word *relationship*.

He gave Adam and Eve one rule. He told them not to eat the fruit from the tree in the center of the garden in which they lived. He wanted them to choose to obey him. He gave them a choice. He didn't want to force them to obey because what kind of love is that?

Adam and Eve broke the one rule they'd been given and ate from the forbidden tree. God was and is, so holy and awesome that he could no longer walk with them because of their betrayal, or you may have heard it as the word *sin*. The sin broke Adam and Eve's perfect world. God didn't break it, they did. And because of it they were cursed and thrown out of paradise.

Outside of the garden, Adam and Eve had children. They were the father and mother of all humanity. But because of their betrayal (or sin), their children were also unable to have a perfect relationship with God. They, and we, are descendants of sin. We did nothing before we were born to deserve this curse, but we were born with it because of the original disobedience.

But God wanted to be close with them, and us, again. Through the generations, he gave rules, performed miracles, and whispered hope into the hearts of humans to bring them back to him. Some listened and had a close relationship with God through their obedience to his laws and Torah, but the reprieve from sin was temporary. Most humans wouldn't listen. They were broken and cursed, unable to fix the problem on their own and unable to follow all of God's laws to the letter, thus leaving them on the outs with their Creator again and again. Only God could create a permanent solution to the problem.

So, God did.

God sent hope to the world in the form of his son, Jesus. Sin equals death, so Jesus sacrificed *his* life, to erase the original betrayal.

To give life.

The Bible says it like this:

"Consequently, just as the result of one trespass was condemnation for all men, so also the result of one act of righteousness was justification that brings life for all men. For just as through the disobedience of the one man the many were made sinners, so also through the obedience of the one man the many will be made righteous." Romans 5:18-19

When Jesus died, he died to erase the death that sin caused. He died so that we wouldn't have to live under the curse brought on by Adam and Eve. He died so we could have life.

Maybe talk of sin seems too serious or preachy. Maybe it doesn't make sense. Instead of getting overwhelmed by big words, let's consider these questions.

Have I ever felt a stirring in my core that begged for love?

Have I ever felt an emptiness inside of me? An ache?

Have I tried to fill the emptiness with a guy, but his love didn't make the ache go away?

Have I tried to make the ache go away by getting a good education and an enviable job?

Have I tried to feel good by subjecting my body to workouts and diets until I looked a certain way?

Have I tried to hide behind makeup or clothes?

Have I given up and accepted the ache?

Remember God's original reason for creating Adam and Eve? He wanted a relationship with them. Because we are each created by God there is a piece inside of us that can only be satisfied with a relationship with him. God made it possible through Jesus to have a lasting close relationship with God without the shame of sin. Jesus died to erase sin and our repentance puts us in right standing with God. In a relationship with him.

The Gospel, or what Christians believe, is believing and accepting the love of God in the form of Jesus to save us from the original sin and fill that empty place inside of us. When we grasp this good news, we are taking hold of hope. We are being thankful to God for saving us.

How to accept God's gift:

It's not enough to know what Jesus did. We must choose to believe and follow him. This is what we call Christianity. Becoming a Christian does not mean we have to wear stuffy clothes to church, become judgmental, or hate anything fun. It means that we decide in our hearts to believe and accept what Jesus did for us, tell someone about our belief, and then spend the rest of our lives trying to live more like Jesus.

Being a Christian is not boring. My friends and I laugh a lot. The main difference is that we look through the world with a different set of glasses. We see hope because we know Jesus has saved us and we want to share that hope with others.

Tips to accept God's gift:

-Pray (which is the same as talking) to God and tell him you believe in him and you want to live your life for him since he gave up his life (Jesus) for you.

-Tell someone who can help you better understand your decision and mentor you along the way.

-Learn all you can about God's love through the Bible, study books, Christians friends, and even nature. God can speak to us in many ways.

-Live! Don't just sit at home and be grateful that you are no longer cursed. Live! Go out and be an example, a ray of hope, for others to see and be attracted to.

-Love well. The best way we can show God that we love him is to love others around us.

CHAPTER 1
EVE

he Seduced Girl

Eve

A 7 Day Study

Before You Start:

Eve was the first woman on earth. Her story can be found by opening the Bible to the very first page.

DAY 1

Girl Read: Genesis Chapter 1:26-31

Girl Life: I developed a life-threatening eating disorder at the age of fifteen and my reflection has been skewed ever since. When I stand in front of the mirror in only my bra and panties, I rarely see the girl I one hundred percent want to look like. The girl I see has wide hips and the little extra skin around her tummy never goes away no matter how much weight she loses.

The reflection I see looking back at me isn't the model of beauty popular culture says I should be. If I wanted to be *that* girl, I'd have to become reacquainted with the eating disorder, quit my job to work out all day, and have surgeries to change the shape of my natural angles. I'd have to change who I am to achieve what I want to look like and that would be a sad way to live.

Girl Do: *Live like you are created in the image of God because you are!*

Our bodies are representations of God in the flesh. We were carefully crafted by the same God who frosted the ocean with waves and the mountains with snow. We shouldn't look at our bodies with disdain or disapproval. We should look at ourselves as beautifully created beings who were made just right. God doesn't make mistakes. He didn't say, "Oops," when he made Adam and Eve.

Instead, we read, "God saw all that he had made, and it was very good." (Genesis 1:31) We are "very good" in God's sight even if we don't look like the girls we follow on social media. When we compare how God made *her* with how God made *us,* we miss out on the beautiful girls we are. The girl's God made us to be.

Girl Ask: Do I live like I am created in the image of God?

DAY 2

Girl Read: Genesis Chapter 2:1-25

Girl Life: My hubby, Mason, doesn't like to cook for himself. I'm pretty sure he lives off of takeout and chips and salsa when I'm out of town. I love the part of our reading today where God desires to give Adam a companion and then makes Eve. Girls and guys were created to be together and complement each other.

For example, I'm the one who makes the meals at our house, but Mason is great at taking care of our finances. In other relationships maybe the girl is the breadwinner and the guy is a stay-at-home dad. In any case, we are meant to work together to make a team like when God made Eve complement Adam. They weren't made to compete. They were made to magnify the strengths of the other.

Girl Do: *Work together with the guy in your life to make a team.*

Eve was created because there was no other created thing perfect enough to be Adam's partner. She was created specifically to fill a role that no creature besides her could fill. She (woman) was made special.

If we have husbands, we should complement their weaknesses with our strengths. If we are dating, we should consider if the man we are dating is someone we want to work together with forever. If we don't mesh well while dating, then we might not if we get married. If we are single, we should learn our strengths so when the right man comes along we know what we have to offer. Girls and guys were not created to compete over who is better at this or stronger at that. We were created to complement each other. To be chocolate and peanut butter—perfect together.

Girl Ask: Am I competing with the guy in my life or complementing him?

DAY 3

Girl Read: Genesis Chapter 3:1-7

Girl Life: When I was between the ages of twelve and fourteen, I looked in the mirror and was seduced by the lie that I'd be prettier if I lost weight. I grabbed ahold of the lie that thinner was better which led me down a dark path that I'm still journeying out of today.

Like Eve was seduced with the idea of being like God, we can be seduced by many things. We can be seduced by body standards, money, influence, social media, careers, boys, food, travel, and other things. If we follow a sparkling lie, we can soon find out that it is an illusion, a mirage, and we might be left stumbling in darkness and pain trying to fix what we broke. Believing that I wasn't pretty destroyed parts of my life

Girl Live: *Don't believe the lie!*

This sounds like simple advice, but when lies are covered in chocolate, sprinkles, and frosting it's hard to see what's underneath. Lies can look good. Like the lie that if we are famous, we will be happy, or if we travel across the globe we will feel fulfilled, or if we lose weight we will feel beautiful. Lies don't play fair. We should bring all the pretty wishes we believe and see if they agree with God's Word. We should seek counsel from friends, a mentor, a family member, a counselor, or a pastor to see if the things we want line up with what God says about us and our worth.

Girl Ask: What lies have I been seduced into believing?

DAY 4

Girl Read: Genesis Chapter 3:8-9

Girl Life: As a prank, I once locked my sisters out of the house. They were not thrilled and went to the woman next door who stormed out of her house to give me a talking to. I quickly unlocked the door and dashed out the back without shoes on and hid in the trees on the hill behind our house as cold mud seeped between my toes.

Today's reading is short but so relevant to us. Adam and Eve hid from God. We are like them because sometimes we hide from God, too. We don't read our Bibles or pray when we feel like we've done something he won't forgive us for, or if we want to do our own thing. We hide, all the while knowing God is God and he knows our hearts and sees us anyway just like he saw Adam and Eve.

Girl Do: *Don't play hide and seek with God.*

No matter where we hide, God will always find us. God walked in the garden with Adam and Eve as a friend walks beside us at the park. He was close enough to touch. When

9

they hid, God found them, and he finds us today no matter where we are. He wants to love us back to himself. He doesn't want us to hide from him. He wants a relationship with us just like he had a relationship with Adam and Eve.

Girl Ask: Am I hiding from God?

DAY 5

Girl Read: Genesis Chapter 3:10-13

Girl Life: I couldn't have been more than five or six when I broke something on my mom's dresser. When she found out, I told her my little sister did it. Guilt berated me as my little sister was yelled at and spanked for the thing I did. Unlike my mom in this instance, God knows when we cast the blame on somebody else. It's easy to point our fingers and blame the person beside us for something we did, but God always knows.

Girl Do: *Don't blame someone else for something you are responsible for.*

When God confronted Adam with his disobedience, he flipped the blame on Eve. We look down on Adam for this, but are we much different? We blame others for the things we do wrong. We blame our friends for making us gossips, traffic for making us late or life for making us busy when we are the ones responsible for those things. We look silly when we try to blame others for things we did, and we look ignorant when we try to hide the truth from God. God knows the truth. There is no reason to blame another. God asked Eve what she had done when he already knew the answer. It's hard to admit when we are wrong but it's the right thing to do.

Girl Ask: Have I ever blamed someone for something I did? Were there still consequences for me?

DAY 6

Girl Read: Genesis Chapter 3:14-19

Girl Life: I was in the room when my niece Astrid was born. My sister's labor lasted all day and I saw her struggle through every stage. She was a rock-star, but all labor is difficult. Because Eve disobeyed God, she had to pay the consequences, and one of those consequences was hard labor. Thanks, Eve . . .

It's crazy to think that thousands of years later we girls are still paying the price for something that was done by the first woman on planet earth. This shows that the mistakes we make don't always affect us, they can also affect those around us or those who come after us.

Girl Do: *Know that there are always consequences for sin (disobeying God).*

Some people call the concept of consequences karma. Others say, "What goes around comes around." Both karma and the saying carry the same concept. The wrong things we do have consequences. Maybe not at the very second, we do the wrong thing, but at some point, we will pay the price for our disobedience. So how do we live differently?

We can avoid consequences by learning the rules. We should learn God's commands and do our best to obey them. It's impossible in our human bodies to get this perfect but because of God's love for us, we should try.

Girl Ask: Have I ever done something wrong that affected not only me but the people around me too?

DAY 7

Girl Read: Genesis Chapter 3:20-24 & 4:1-2

Girl Life: I love my parents even though they punished me. My mom and dad are two of my closest friends. Even though God cursed Adam & Eve and banished them from Eden, Eve still recognized God as her helper after giving birth to her first son. I think Eve still loved and respected God based on the faithfulness her son Cain and other close descendants showed God. I believe she taught her children to fear and respect God. Although we do wrong and we must suffer the aftermath we can still love those who correct us.

Girl Do: *Know that regardless of the punishment God may place on you for your disobedience, you can still trust him to be loving and faithful.*

God does not throw around curses and punishments for no reason. He doesn't do it because he enjoys it. God loves us and wants us to have the best life. He puts fences (rules) around certain areas to keep us from hurting ourselves. Just like our parents told us not to run with sharp objects or place our hands on a burning stovetop, God only has our best interest in mind when he gives us rules. God didn't want to make Adam and Eve's life boring by giving them a rule. He wanted them to flourish under his directions. He wants the same thing for us.

Girl Ask: Do I believe that God's rules are for my good?

A LETTER TO THE SEDUCED GIRL

Dear Seduced Girl,

I've been where you are and believed the sugar-coated lies. .
.

Maybe I don't need God as much as I thought.

I'd be more beautiful if I changed the way I looked. Maybe God didn't know what he was doing when he created me.

It's just one night with this boy. Maybe God didn't mean it when he created sex for a husband and wife.

I can't afford to help other people. Maybe God doesn't see how busy I am or how little money I have.

Girl, I know it's easy to get wrapped up in thoughts like this and wonder if God has your best interest in mind. This is the age-old seduction that makes us wonder, *did God really say. . . ?* (Genesis 3:1) Believing lies is sometimes so much easier than living in truth. It's easier to do the things we want to rather than following the carefully laid out plans God has for us.

Dear seduced girl, you are not alone. Like Eve, you have been created in the image of God. You are a beautiful created daughter of the same God who created sunsets, blooming magnolias, mountain peaks, and sweet summer fruit. You are not an accident or a mistake. God made you with a beautiful purpose in mind, and yet, you are tempted to believe lies.

The enemy of God wants to distract you from the things God wants for you. The enemy wants you to question if God loves you or if God knows what's best for you. The enemy wants you to believe his lies and fall into his traps.

Many of us seduced girls have fallen and had to fight our way back to the light and truth. This can be a long and painful journey. But you know what? You can do it! Seriously, girl, you can! Regardless of what you have done God still loves you and he still calls you his daughter. He wants to show you the truth and help you fight the lies you believe. He loves you more than you can imagine, and he wants to see you set free from the seductive lies of the enemy.

Cling to God. You can do this.

From,

A Girl Who Cares

CHAPTER 2

DEBORAH & JAEL

$\mathcal{T}$he Warrior Girls

DEBORAH & JAEL

A 3 DAY STUDY

BEFORE YOU START:

Deborah and Jael's story took place in the Old Testament which means the events took place before Jesus came to earth. Years before Deborah and Jael, God delivered the nation of Israel out of slavery and placed them in his promised land. He took the people by the hand like a daddy with his little girl and taught them how to live. God's number one rule was that the people love him first and foremost. But they didn't. They turned away from him, so God placed judges (leaders) among them to point them back to him and his greatness.

DAY 1

Girl Read: Judges Chapter 4:1-10

Girl Life: In elementary school, we played a game called Boys vs. Girls. If we were tagged, we had to sit in a little cave on the playground. One of my childhood friends was the leader of the boy's team and I was the leader of the girl's team. The school was small, and the boys outnumbered the girls, but we ran the playground like warriors. The Bible also has a smaller tribe of girls who lead, but when they do, huge things happen. Deborah was an esteemed leader in a time when women didn't have prominent roles in society. She used her leadership to point people towards God.

Girl Do: *Lead people toward God.*

Girls can lead people too. Deborah led in the book of Judges and Esther led in the book of Esther. There are two ways to lead people: towards God or away from God. In the books of 1 & 2 Kings, Queen Jezebel led people toward idol worship. If we want to mirror strong leaders like Deborah and Esther, we must seek God. Some ways to seek God are reading the Bible, worshiping, journaling, studying, reading books by girls who know more than us, and joining communities of women who love God.

Girl Ask: Do I lead people toward God?

DAY 2

Girl Read: Judges Chapter 4:11-24

Girl Life: Sometimes I feel like I need to be speaking God's truth to crowds of people, publishing books, or being a leader to make a difference. But Jael's story proves otherwise. God used Jael for greatness right where she was. When I get discouraged about where I am for this season, I remember my husband and how God has called me to be a wife. I remember the students I mentor and how I am called to walk alongside them. I don't have to have a huge platform or travel to a different country on a mission trip to make a difference. God can use me right where I am. He can use you right where you are, too.

Girl Do: *Follow God's leading right where you are.*

Jael was a wife at home one moment and a warrior the next. She didn't leave her house to serve God. She served him from where she was. We can fulfill God's purpose for our lives whether we are stay-at-home moms, boss ladies, students, or wives. The important thing is that we do what

God calls us to do. If God calls us to hug kids on a mission trip to Guatemala, we should go. If God calls us to start a small business, we should take steps to obey. If God calls us to move away from home, we should go. If God calls us to make a meal for our husband, we should cook. If God calls us to be patient with our child and teach them the right way to live, we should do it.

Girl Ask: What has God called me to do from right where I am?

DAY 3

Girl Read: Judges Chapter 5:1-31

Girl Life: I like to say, "Thank you, Jesus," as a whispered prayer when I think of all he's given me. I say the same words when he helps me accomplish something or I feel near to him. Judges Chapter 5 is 31 verses of Deborah saying, "Thank you, God," in a song. Like my simple three words, her song is a response to her thankfulness for all God has done for her and through her.

Girl Do: *Thank God, girl!*

We have so much to be thankful for. Our homes, the food we eat, clean water, education, jobs, friends and family, and the freedom to worship God. Find something to thank God for today. Already today I am thankful for slow Saturday mornings, my delicious tea, and a beautiful home. If you want, you could try writing a poem or song to God about how thankful you are or about how great he is. If you need inspiration re-read Deborah's song or flip forward in your Bible to the book of Psalms.

Girl Ask: What can I thank God for today?

A LETTER TO THE WARRIOR GIRL

Dear Warrior Girl,

Don't push your calling aside because you think a woman cannot make a difference or fight battles. You are a strong and beautiful woman because God has created you in such a way. You may not be capable on your own, but when you grab hold of God's hand, you can win battles.

Remember, Warrior Girl, that fighting a war is hard work. It's fun to call ourselves warriors but harder to stand firm against the bullets that are laser-focused at our hearts. Girls fight many battles. We fight for our families, our friends, our dreams, our hopes, and our very lives. We know strength, but weakness lurks within our shadows, whispering that we are not good enough or strong enough to win against the struggle we are facing. But God's strength is made perfect in our weakness, 2 Corinthians 12:9-10 says,

"'. . . He said to me, "My grace is sufficient for you, for my power is made perfect in weakness."

Therefore I will boast all the more gladly about my weaknesses, so that Christ's power may rest on me . . . For when I am weak, then I am strong.'

Remember, it's HIS strength, not ours. And after the battle, it is God to whom we should be thanking. Not ourselves.

But friend, we don't only fight external challenges, but also *in*ternal ones. We fight anxiety, depression, fear, memories, and self-doubt. Our friends and family may not see the scars from these wars as plainly as they might see others, but they are real to us. Girl, if you are fighting an internal war, know this, you are *not* alone. The war of our minds can be spiritual as well as mental.

"'For our struggle is not against flesh and blood, but against the rulers, against the authorities, against the powers of this dark world and against the spiritual forces of evil in the heavenly realms.'" Ephesians 6:12

There is an unseen war happening right now for your soul. A war against good and evil, darkness and light. We must fight for the light to win in our lives. Fighting internal battles can sometimes be harder than fighting external ones. There are several ways we can fight these internal battles.

1. Seek God's word and his wisdom. Fight the lies and fears you believe with his truth. Read the Bible, pray, find a mentor. However you choose to do it, seek God, girl.

2. Tell someone you are struggling. Don't hide your battle because of shame or fear. We can't always fight these battles alone. Remember, armies are made of many warriors, not just one.

3. Get help, whether that be a spiritual mentor or mental health professional for mental disorders like depression,

OCD, PTSD, personality disorders, eating disorders, or schizophrenia.

Warrior Girl, you are awesome. You are a beautiful fighter and you can make a difference. Maybe to fight you must go to war like Deborah with Barak, or maybe you need to stay right where you are and fight the battle God has placed directly in front of you.

Fight on, girl.

From,

A Girl Who Cares

CHAPTER 3
RUTH

he Devoted Girl

RUTH

A 6 DAY STUDY

BEFORE YOU START:

The story of Ruth is the first of only two books in the Bible named after women. The second is Esther. The book of Ruth is only 4 chapters long and has two main characters: Ruth and Naomi. The story took place in the Old Testament. Ruth was the great-grandma of King David.

DAY 1

Girl Read: Ruth Chapter 1:1-18

Girl Life: My life was turned upside-down when my husband Mason received an innocent email. The email was from a large company in California scouting for new hires.

"It wouldn't hurt to apply," I said.

At the time I was happily settled in Florida. We'd been married for over five years and I was scribbling out adoption applications on the weekends. I was excited about my future and I felt safe and happy where I was. But then Mason received the job and all arrows pointed to California. A cross country move may seem like a grand adventure when your twenty-something, but I didn't want the adventure. I wanted to stay safe at home. I wanted to stay in Florida. But with God's nudging and my love and devotion for Mason, I tearfully packed up my things and followed him to California.

Girl Do: *Live a devoted life.*

Ruth also left the home she was familiar with to follow someone she loved to a new place. She was devoted to Naomi like I am devoted to God and Mason. Devotion doesn't mean we have to move from one place to another. Devotion can mean staying faithful to a hurting friend, choosing to love and respect our husbands during tough periods, sticking with family through hard times, or staying true to who we are. Our ultimate devotion should be to God. Ruth chose to be devoted to both Naomi and God. Choosing God should be the blueprint for our lives of devotion.

Girl Ask: What or who am I devoted to?

DAY 2

Girl Read: Ruth Chapter 1:19-22

Girl Life: Sometimes I have flashbacks from when I struggled with an eating disorder. I remember sitting in the adolescent hospital ward with other broken kids, the needles in my arm to take my vitals, hearing horror stories fellow occupants told of past trauma, group therapy, medications, and feeling more like a case number than a human.

Ruth and Naomi had painful pasts, too. The men they loved died and left them in a culture where it was difficult to be a woman alone. While I am sure they didn't forget the love of the past, they chose to walk into their future. They could have wallowed in sadness and done nothing. But instead, even Naomi who carried bitterness moved forward by journeying back to Bethlehem.

Girl Do: *Leave your past behind you.*

We don't have to forget the things in our past, but we can't let them control our present. There can be both heart-wrenching and wonderful things behind us. The trick is to find the good, the bad, and the ugly and turn them into something useful right now instead of being swamped in yesterday. While my past is filled with pain, it is also filled with love and home. I live very far away from my family. It's difficult to not live in the past, wanting my old friends and the closeness I had with my family.

But God has placed us right where we are, and we can't live in yesterday when he is calling us to live in today.

Girl Ask: Am I living in today or yesterday?

DAY 3

Girl Read: Ruth Chapter 2:1-17

Girl Life: While they would have loved to, my parents could not financially support me or my sisters for college. I found a job at a jewelry store and paid for each college semester I attended without loan assistance. It was important to my growth to work for the money I used to attend college. It cultivated a sense of pride in what I accomplished. Working made it possible to go to college which just so happened to be the place where I met my future husband. If Ruth hadn't gone to the barley fields, she never would have met Boaz.

Girl Do: *Put in the work.*

We can't expect wonderful things to fall from heaven like rainwater. God supplies us with many things, but there are other things we must work for. Working opens many doors and avenues in life, from better-paying jobs to meeting new friends or finding new things we're passionate about.

Have you ever read Proverbs 31:10-31 about the noble wife? Whew. Reading about how much she worked for what she had is both inspiring and exhausting. But the verses are also proof that women should work, too! Whether we work at an office or work from home raising our kids and being a housewife, work is important.

Girl Ask: What good things have come from my working?

DAY 4

Girl Read: Ruth Chapter 2:18-23

Girl Life: I remember sitting on the beach with my best friend as a kid and saying, "Ugh, I will *never* be like my mom. She doesn't understand." We both agreed . . .

But then we grew up and realized that our moms were amazing, and we wanted to be *just* like them. As the saying goes, we were "young and dumb." We obeyed our moms out of obligation, not because we wanted to. Now my mom is one of the first people I go to for advice. She's who I call when I don't feel good or when I want to talk through something. Many times, older women in our lives can see things clearer than us. They see a bigger picture where we are only seeing our little world. Ruth listened to Naomi's advice and didn't stray from Boaz's field.

Girl Do: *Be humble and obedient to the wise women in your life.*

I'm sure we can each think of a wiser older woman in our life. She might not be old, but she's older than we are. There are several women in my life: my mom, my mother-in-law, my second mom/mentor, my grandma, my aunts, sister-in-law, and some of my friends. Listening to the advice of women older and more experienced is wise. We can't do life on our own and a great place to look for advice is from the women who have walked before us.

Girl Ask: What women in my life can I go to for advice?

DAY 5

Girl Read: Ruth Chapter 3:1-18

Girl Life: I heard the words at church. I read the words between the pages of paperback books about dating and purity. I heard them spoken from the mouths of people I looked up to.

"Don't ever be alone with the guy you are dating. Go out in groups. Don't do anything that would lead to sex. Don't have sex before you are married."

Mason and I waited until marriage for the bedroom stuff, but we spent a lot of time alone together. We did dating (mostly) right. Yes, we had a few rough patches and did a few things we probably shouldn't have, but I didn't make myself as vulnerable as Ruth did when she went to a man in the middle of the night in a culture where women had very few rights or protections. There are times to have fun and let loose but also times to be wise and not put ourselves in bad situations.

Girl Do: *Be wise, not reckless.*

I don't believe in telling girls to, "Not hold hands," or "Don't kiss," or "Don't be alone together," because I think each relationship and girl is different. Ultimately what we do in our relationships will be between us, God, and the guy. While there may not be a "one size fits all" as far as dating rules, there are steps we can take as Christian girls to protect our hearts and our bodies.

1. Go to God first - When we have a close relationship with God we will be in a better position to discern the difference between a wise and reckless decision. The reference to a redeemer in these passages refers to guidelines God put into place to protect families. When Ruth went to Boaz, she was requesting him to honor the law of God.

2. Trust the wisdom of older and wiser women - We already touched on this in yesterday's study, but it is so important. We may hate to admit it, but sometimes our Moms, big sisters, mentors, or girlfriends may be wiser than we are in certain situations. We should get advice as Ruth did from Naomi, before making big relationship decisions.

Girl Ask: Am I setting myself up to make wise choices in my dating life or am I being reckless?

DAY 6

Girl Read: Ruth Chapter 4:1-22

Girl Life: Six and a half years ago I was hit with fear so deep and so personal that it caused me to hide in the bathroom at work to take deep breaths. The bathroom fan whirred as I closed my eyes and tried to calm myself. Fear had such a hold on me that I could hardly function. I asked my spiritual mentors for help. The fear didn't just disappear. I had to continue forward despite the fear while reminding myself of truth. This experience with fear was the second most difficult thing I faced in my life up to that point besides my eating disorder. I still consider it one of the greatest challenges I've experienced. But I learned in that time of terrifying uncertainty that the only way to live is in God's hand, trusting him with everything. Now, instead of fighting hard times, I lean into them, knowing that God has something great on the other side.

Girl Do: *Let God take care of you and see what he can do with your life.*

Ruth left everything with only trust in Naomi and God. This led her to a man who chose to love her and care for her and give her children. If we flip ahead in the Bible to Matthew 1:5 we see that Ruth is mentioned in the lineage of Jesus Christ. Not only did her trust and leaning on God give her a path through hard times in life, but it also gave her a spot in the pages of history. When we trust God with everything, follow him, and move in his direction we give him space to move in amazing ways in our lives.

Girl Ask: Do I let God take care of me or do I try to control and fix everything?

A LETTER TO THE DEVOTED GIRL

Dear Devoted Girl,

You are amazing and sweet for having such a caring heart. You love and pour out of yourself for those you love. People know you as faithful, loving, and caring. The world needs girls like you!

But girl, can I ask you a question?

Who are you most devoted to? Is it a family member, a friend, a child, a lover? And after reading the book of Ruth, do you think you should shift your devotion to be first and foremost to God?

No matter how much you love and are devoted to a person, they cannot fulfill that piece of your soul that cries to be connected to God. The people you are most devoted to do not know the deepest parts of your heart. You can share everything with them and they will still not know *everything*. They don't know you. Who your soul is. Who you are. You are so complex and detailed that only your Creator can know you best. You are known.

My second question is this.

Can you be first and foremost devoted to God?

Since God is the Creator that knows you best, it makes sense to choose him to be your number one devotion. This is hard sometimes because you cannot touch, help, hug, and have a human conversation with God. It is hard to be devoted to someone you cannot see. It's even harder to be devoted to this same being above every other.

Nobody gets this right. We all put other things in front of God, but it should be our goal to be devoted to God first and foremost.

Ruth was devoted to Naomi and God, teaching us that it is beautiful to be devoted to both people and God. But it makes sense to be most devoted to the One who created us. Devotion to God will feed your soul.

Be devoted to God by seeking him in everything. Look to his word to understand who he is. Seek counsel from spiritual mentors who can help you cultivate your relationship with God. Talk to him. Seek him. Have a relationship. Be devoted.

Some of you might be devoted to someone who does not uplift you. Regarding this, I must tell you that you are worth so much more than someone who does not treat you with respect and love as a daughter of God. Be wise in who you devote yourself to.

Devote yourself to God first. Trust him. And see where he will lead you.

From,

A Girl Who Cares

CHAPTER 4
MARY

he Trusting Girl

MARY

A 6 DAY STUDY

BEFORE YOU START:

Mary was the mother of Jesus Christ, Savior of the world.
Historians believed that Mary was in her young teens when
she became pregnant with Jesus.

DAY 1

Girl Read: Luke Chapter 1:26-38

Girl Life: My husband and I sat across a restaurant table and discussed the pros and cons of giving away one of our possessions that could be sold for a decent amount of money. When I first mentioned the idea, Mason turned it down, giving away something we could sell would be crazy. Why would we do that? But I felt this tug on my heart that we should give the item away. The more we talked, the more we both came to peace with the crazy idea. I one hundred percent believed that the nudge on my heart to give the item away was from God.

The things God inspires us to do may not always make sense, but the peace both Mason and I felt after we made the decision confirmed it was from God. We have not once regretted giving away the possession we could have sold. Some may call us crazy, but God doesn't.

Girl Do: *Trust God even when it seems crazy.*

I doubt many of us would be as willing as Mary to accept an unplanned pregnancy. But Mary didn't hesitate. She accepted the crazy idea of being a teen mom without having sex both quickly and humbly. She trusted God's plan without asking a dozen questions first. It's not like there were pregnant virgins in abundance. No girl had taken that path before and none have since, but she trusted anyway. We can follow in Mary's footsteps when we accept those seemingly crazy ideas that God gives us and follow through.

Girl Ask: What would I do if God asked me to do something crazy?

DAY 2

Girl Read: Luke Chapter 1:39-56

Girl Life: I wore an ivory wedding dress with a beaded bodice and elegant train. I was as calm as a scared girl could be. Mason and I had a lot of ups and downs before our wedding day. A paralyzing fear almost kept me from giving him a second chance, but God worked on my heart and I felt that marrying Mason was the right thing. And I really, *really* wanted to. I told God multiple times that I'd be just fine ditching the relationship (because I was scared) but he pressed me forward with gentle steady love. I've now been married for over six years and I still totally believe that marrying Mason was/is God's plan for my life. I may have been terrified, but God gave me strength and peace.

Girl Do: *Trust that God's plan is good even when it's scary.*

Getting pregnant out of wedlock in biblical times was punishable by death. But instead of hiding at home with the shades drawn Mary traveled to visit a cousin and then praised God! The existence of a baby in her womb could have meant her death but instead of being scared, she trusted God enough to praise him during a potentially terrifying circumstance. We try so hard to be our own gods that it's hard to trust the true God. Trusting in scary situations is well...scary. But God is with us in every moment.

Girl Ask: Am I willing to trust God in scary situations?

DAY 3

Girl Read: Luke Chapter 2:1-20

Girl Life: A few months before she was diagnosed with cancerous brain tumors, I had the privilege of spending almost two weeks with my grandma-in-law along with Mason's family. Grandma and I had many sweet conversations about God and family. None of us had any idea our time with her was dwindling. But now, two and a half years since that cherished time, and eight months since her passing, I still treasure those days with her. I remember walking museum grounds with her, learning to make traditional Armenian food, and simply sitting together on the couch.

Girl Do: *Treasure the special moments.*

Mary set an example for us by observing and treasuring moments (Luke 2:19). Life can go fast, but we can choose to slow down and cherish the moments. Some moments won't seem as grand as shepherd's relaying stories of angels, but they can still be special. I live over two thousand miles from my family and hometown. My memories of simply sitting in the living room of my childhood home as a family are moments I treasure. We can practice pausing our day or our minds and live in the moment. It only takes a minute to take note of the sight of a sunset, the smell of freshly baked cookies, the touch of a loved one, the sound of the wind in the trees, or the taste of a kiss.

Girl Ask: What happened recently that I want to treasure?

DAY 4

Girl Read: Luke Chapter 2:21-40

Girl Life: I walked into the maternity ward of the hospital with my mom and my pregnant little sister. She'd been having contractions for over twenty-four hours and it was time for her to be induced and deliver the baby. She handled labor like a pro and birthed her baby with the help of an epidural eight hours after we arrived. She didn't get the epidural right away. She suffered through most of her laboring before having it administered. I hope I always remember the look on her face when her daughter was placed on her chest. With great pain came great joy.

Girl Do: *Understand that sometimes there will be pain mixed with joy.*

Babies bring joy. It's hard not to smile when we see them. Their big watery eyes, chubby cheeks, and gleeful smiles bring happiness to our hearts. Eight days after he was born, Mary was told that her son was the salvation of Israel, but also, *"a sword will pierce your own soul,"* (Luke 2:35). She was warned that the joy she had in her arms would one day break her heart. We know that this prophecy foreshadows the sacrificial death of Jesus on the cross. Because of the absolute trust Mary had for God in Luke chapter 1, I think we can assume that Mary would have chosen the joy mixed with pain from the moment she heard God's call on her life if given the choice. Mary loved her son, but she loved and was faithful to God.

Girl Ask: What in life has brought me both joy and pain?

DAY 5

Girl Read: Luke Chapter 2:41-52

Girl Life: When I was a teen and needed help recovering from my eating disorder, I went to live in a home that helped girls in situations like mine. It was called Mercy Multiplied. When I remember my time at Mercy, I feel a deep sense of peace and love. In my mind's eye, I can still see the large entryway with ceilings as high as the second floor. I see the staircases leading to the second-floor bedrooms and the gathering room. I see the kitchen and dining rooms. In my heart and mind, I know God touched me there. I felt him in all of those rooms. His presence lived within the walls and healed the girls inside. Over eleven years later, I know that he is still close. He always has been.

Girl Do: *Know where to find God.*

As a teen, I found God at Mercy Multiplied. In our reading today, Mary found Jesus in the temple, which would be comparable to a church today. In most of the Bible, the place where God could be found was the temple. It was where his Spirit lived. But when Jesus died on the cross years later, he broke the barrier between God and humans. He made it so that we could find God within us. We don't have to consult a priest or be within the walls of a church to hear from God. We can pray to him from our souls and know he is close. God can be found in churches, but he can also be found in sunsets, friendships, mountains, living rooms, and within the hearts of you and me.

Girl Ask: Where do you find God?

DAY 6

Girl Read: John Chapter 19:25-27

Girl Life: I watched my mother-in-law care for her mom as her body grew frail and slowly stopped working. She took care of her mom in ways I'm not sure I could. And she did it with a smile. She knew her mom was terminally ill, but she didn't let that diagnosis keep her from lavishing her love on her mother every day, multiple times a day. She sat, prayed, cried, and laughed at her mother's bedside in the months before her death, knowing that soon she would pass, but not wanting to miss a minute with her. She didn't let the fear of loss keep her from continuing to love her with all her heart and actions.

Girl Do: *Love when it hurts.*

Mary stood at the foot of the cross as her son was dying. She didn't look away. She loved him until his last breath. Loving is hard when we know it will hurt, and girl, it *will* hurt. The people we love will fail us, and yes, all people die. But failure and death should not keep us from loving. We can't live a life without love because we are afraid of being hurt. Remember day 4 of this study of Mary? There will be pain mixed with joy. Although we will face great pain in life, we will also have days of gladness. Don't be afraid to love, girl. We have been created by a loving God. We were made to love and be loved.

Girl Ask: Do I love when it hurts or do I run away?

A LETTER TO THE TRUSTING GIRL

Dear Trusting Girl,

Maybe your trusting heart has gotten you into trouble in the past. Did trusting the wrong person hurt you? Was your trust taken advantage of? Dear girl, having a trusting heart is not naive or weak, it is strength. It takes great faith to trust, and even greater faith to trust in the things we are uncertain of.

You may have put your trust in the wrong person but trusting God will never steer you wrong.

Proverbs 3: 5-6 says:

"Trust in the LORD with all your heart

and lean not on your own

understanding;

in all your ways acknowledge him,

and he will make your paths

straight."

Trusting God will no doubt take you on some wild journeys, but don't fear or doubt when you let God lead you. God sees the bigger picture. He takes us down roads we couldn't imagine because our vision is too distorted or nearsighted.

Mary is a great example of a trusting woman of God. She accepted risks and trusted God wholeheartedly. She didn't doubt God when he told her she would become pregnant. She believed in God enough to trust him with all of her heart.

So, girl, trust God with all your heart. Never stop. Believe he loves you. Trust he cares. And follow him.

From,

A Girl Who Cares

CHAPTER 5

HANNAH

he Bullied Girl

Hannah

A 4 Day Study

Before You Start:

Hannah was a wife in the Old Testament to a man named Elkanah who had two wives. Her story is the beginning of the two books of the Bible titled 1 & 2, Samuel. Her story sets the stage for Israel's first king, Saul, and later, King David.

DAY 1

Girl Read: 1 Samuel Chapter 1:1-17

Girl Life: My middle school years were a nightmare. I never felt like I fit in. I received weird looks from girls, and I swear some of them whispered about me. I attended a very small country school where bullying was not a big issue and I was blessed to not grow up in the age of social media or online bullying. But there was still bullying. Kids who were different were singled out and verbally beaten. In high school, I was called many unkind (or inappropriate) names because I was a girl who liked to hang out with boys.

Girl Do: *Bring your hurts to God.*

In the passage we read today, Hannah was bullied by the second wife of her husband. Let's not dig too deeply into why this man had two wives and focus on Hannah's reaction to the bullying of Peninnah. She was fed-up with the hate and went straight to God. She didn't spew hurt back, she pleaded to the only one she knew could change her situation. Bullying is not just something that happens in middle and high school hallways. It happens to adults too. Maybe the bullying that we endure is online, in person, or through text. No matter where it's coming from or who is the perpetrator, we can bring it to God.

Girl Ask: Is there a hurt related to bullying that I need to bring to God?

DAY 2

Girl Read: 1 Samuel Chapter 1:18-28

Girl Life: I was excited to get married, but also terrified. I knew how serious the promises I would make to Mason and God were. I think Hannah treated the vow she made to God like a marriage vow. She wasn't trying to manipulate God into giving her the desire of her heart. Her dedication fascinates me. Why would she promise to give away the thing she prayed for? But not only did she promise to give God her son, she actually gave God her son. She brought him to the temple (or church) to serve God. Notice the title of the book of the Bible we are reading.

Samuel.

Hannah's son Samuel not only became a great leader in Israel but also had two books of the Bible named after him.

Girl Do: *Keep your word.*

You never know what God will do with your promise. For Hannah, he made her son into a prophet. She didn't cling tightly to what God gave her and instead gave it back to him. The people, things, and dreams God gives us are his to begin with. When we give back to God what he has blessed us with we are giving back something that already belongs to him.

Girl Ask: Do I keep my promises?

DAY 3

Girl Read: I Samuel Chapter 2:1-11

Girl Life: I grew up knowing God's love, but I truly discovered God's love in the hallways of a home for girls where I sought healing for my eating disorder. After answered prayers and an overflowing of acceptance from God, I grew confident that he could do the same for other girls in hard situations. God's greatness was made known to me by him putting me back together. Like my wanting to share God's greatness, Hannah couldn't keep quiet about the greatness of God. Instead of weeping when she brought her son to God, she praised him because she knew how amazing he is.

Girl Do: *Be confident in God's greatness.*

If you haven't experienced the love and awesomeness of God yourself, know that it is there through the stories of the girls in the Bible. God's greatness is real, amazing, and grand. He cares so much for you even when it feels like he is far away. Hannah sang a song, but maybe you could write a poem or a few words that describe God's greatness in your own life. Know that God is great!

Girl Ask: Am I confident in God's greatness?

DAY 4

Girl Read: I Samuel Chapter 2:18-21

Girl Life: I've been married for over six years and being faithful is not easy. I don't mean that in a sense of being tempted toward other men. I mean that staying loving, kind, and giving can be difficult when you live with someone every day. It's hard not to let life get in the way of the joy that can be a part of marriage. Continued faithfulness is hard. We must choose to show up for the difficult things. Hannah was faithful. She didn't stop going to offer a sacrifice to God each year because it would be painful to see the son she dedicated to God. She went and visited Samuel and worshiped God. Then God gave her more children to replace the one she gave to him.

Girl Do: *Be faithful to God.*

Sometimes it's not easy to dedicate our time to God when there are so many other things on our minds. I'm sure there are dozens of things you could be doing right now instead of reading your Bible. But today you showed up. You read

God's word. You were faithful in spending time with Him. We know faithfulness to God is the right thing, but it can be hard. Keep being faithful to God in whatever way he calls you.

Girl Ask: Is there a time in my life I stopped being faithful to God because it was hard?

A LETTER TO THE BULLIED GIRL

Dear Bullied Girl,

Don't believe the hurtful things a friend, acquaintance, parent, sibling, boyfriend, or husband have said to you. If what they said does not line up with what God says about you then it is not true. You have value. You have meaning. You are not the sum of the hurtful things that have been said to you.

You have been thoughtfully placed on this earth. (Psalm 139:13-18)

You are not a mistake. (Ephesians 1:4-6)

You are a child of God. (1 John 3:1)

You are loved. (Romans 5:8)

Your life has meaning. (Ephesians 2:10)

You are cared for and beautiful. (Matthew 6:28-29)

You are created in God's image. (Genesis 1:27)

Your heart is known. (1 Samuel 16:7)

71

Girl, I want to share a few simple words that God spoke to my heart. I don't remember what I was feeling, but I remember being in church during either worship, prayer, or the message. I remember these words being spoken to my heart, "I thought you were worth saving."

I almost burst into tears. Me? Worth saving?

This is true of you, too. Jesus thought you were worth saving. He lived and died for *you*. You have amazing value to him. You are his precious girl. No matter what anyone says to you, you are loved.

It's hard to remember (and believe) that we are loved when terrible things are being said or written about us, but we can learn from Hannah to bring those things directly to God. God heard Hannah and he will hear you too. Yes, you.

Bring your hurts to God. Remind yourself of his love for you. Know that you are not a mistake, ugly, or useless. You are not a waste of space. The world would *not* be better without you. You are meant to walk this earth right now. You are amazing, girl. You are loved.

Bring your hurts to God, girl. Let him heal you. Don't forget that *you* were worth saving.

From,

A Girl Who Cares

CHAPTER 6
BATHSHEBA

he Beautiful Girl

B<small>ATHSHEBA</small>

A 3 D<small>AY</small> S<small>TUDY</small>

B<small>EFORE</small> Y<small>OU</small> S<small>TART</small>:

King David was the second king of Israel. God said that David was a man after his heart. David was a good man who loved God but made some very bad choices. Bathsheba was the wife of one of David's most trusted and elite warriors.

N<small>OTE</small>:

People are divided on whether the story of David and Bathsheba is an epic love story or one of victimization.

73

Some think that Bathsheba was trying to get David's attention while others think she was used. The Bible does not tell us the condition of Bathsheba's heart. I see her as more of a victim and this study is based on my personal feelings regarding that. I think that David and Bathsheba may have come to form a real loving bond, but I'm not sure I believe it began that way. Feel free to dig into some of the literature out there and form your own opinion.

It's important to know that God redeemed both David from sin and Bathsheba from brokenness. Bathsheba was given the privilege of being the mother of the wisest and wealthiest man to ever walk the planet while David's sin was made known and he paid the consequences for his poor decisions for the rest of his life. David was called a man after God's heart. He was quick to repent of his mistakes and make things right with God.

DAY 1

Girl Read: 2 Samuel Chapter 11:1-27

Girls Life: I was sixteen years old the first time I received unwanted attention from a man. I stood in a doorway of a public place greeting people. There was a gap in time when I was the only one standing there. As I greeted an older man, he grabbed me in a very inappropriate way while making lewd comments about my body. I froze in place, so surprised that I couldn't react or stop him. Through the years I have continued to attract unwanted male attention that has left me feeling embarrassed, scared, and dirty. The very existence of every girl makes her beautiful because she is created in the image of God. Unfortunately, there are men in each of our lives whether they be friends or strangers that don't treat us with respect. Like Bathsheba, our bodies and our beauty are abused or used.

Girl Do: *Recognize that you are not responsible for the bad choices the men around you make.*

God has given each of us free choice and some people use that to take advantage of others. This is wrong. If you have ever received unwanted, inappropriate, or abusive attention from a man it was not your fault. You are not the cause of a man's actions. Sin and tragedy are born through the heart of the person who perpetrates the crime, not the victim.

Girl, know that it was not your fault.

Girl Ask: Am I carrying the blame for something that was done to me?

DAY 2

Girl Read: 2 Samuel Chapter 12:1-31

Girl Life: When I struggled with anorexia as a teenager I cried helplessly in my dark bedroom. I didn't see a way out of the darkness inside of me. There was no light. But when God restored my health and began the healing of my mind, he also made those broken parts of my past beautiful. He helped me leverage my pain into something he could use to help other girls who were going through the same thing. While the Bible does not tell us if Bathsheba loved David, (many think they did love each other) we do know that God used her pain for good.

Girl Do: *Know that God makes broken things beautiful.*

God makes beauty out of brokenness. Bathsheba was used by David but that was not the end of her story. In 1 Chronicles 28 David announced that Solomon, the second son of Bathsheba, would be king after him. It was common practice in Biblical times for the firstborn to be king in the event of his death. Bathsheba was not David's first wife and there were several sons born before her son. In this case, God chose Solomon, to be king after David. The pain that Bathsheba went through and the relationship she had with King David resulted in her being the mother of Solomon who later became known as the wealthiest and wisest man to ever walk the earth. God can use our bad choices for his glory and make beauty out of brokenness.

Girl Ask: Has God made beauty out of any of my brokenness?

DAY 3

Girl Read: I Kings Chapter 1:11-40

Girl Life: The greatest fights of my life have not happened on dirt strewn battlefields, in the courtrooms of a palace, or inside humble homes. They happened inside my mind. The promises that God has whispered to my heart and the truth that has been spoken over my life has been threatened by only me and my lack of faith. I've fought self-hatred and crippling fear within the walls of my head. Bathsheba walked palace corridors to plead with David to give her son what God promised. She fought for a kingdom while I've fought for freedom from darkness and fear. God promised that Bathsheba's son would be king. God promised me that I would live. God's promises are worth fighting for.

Girl Do: *If your promise from God is threatened, fight for it.*

Christian girls are not meant to sit on the sidelines and let people trample over their God-given dreams and gifts. God has called us all to fight against evil. Sometimes we may have to fight like Bathsheba by speaking up about what God said. Other times our fighting may be by praying the word of God. Fighting against evil can take many forms. God can use girls, like Bathsheba, to guide and shape our history. Maybe we won't be responsible for a kingdom, but we can be responsible for the things God has put in our lives right here, right now.

Girl Ask: Is there a promise I need to fight for today?

A LETTER TO THE BEAUTIFUL GIRL

Dear Beautiful Girl,

First, I must say that if you are a girl and you are reading this, you are beautiful. You may not feel beautiful or see yourself as beautiful based on what you see on social media, in your friends, or in the world around you. But girl, you are BEAUTIFUL!

As a beautiful girl, you face the harsh reality of the broken world around you. You may have been left the victim of a man who used his strength or power to take something from you or make you feel like your beauty is more of a curse than a blessing. You might have been left feeling inadequate, ashamed, dirty, used, or worth only what your body can offer. I've felt this way simply walking down the sidewalk while men screamed at me from the windows of their cars. I've felt this way in public places when men have looked at me longer than they should. In those moments I've wanted to crawl into a hole and hide.

On day 1 of this study about Bathsheba, I said this, but I will say it again. You are *not* responsible for what has been done

81

or said to you. It does not matter what you were wearing or where you were. What happened to you, or was said to you, is not your fault.

Regardless of how this world makes you feel, you have amazing value. You are worth more to God than you give yourself credit for. You are worth his most precious possession. You are worth His son. *That's* how much he loves you. He loves you enough to trade Jesus for you.

Remember, beautiful girl, when you look in the mirror, you are created in the image of God. When someone hurts you or disrespects you, God sees. God *cares*. He created you the way you are for a reason. You carry a piece of God inside of you as a part of his creation. Don't let how others treat you cause you to doubt your worth.

You are amazing.

You are beautiful.

You are strong.

You are chosen.

You were created.

You have a purpose.

From,

A Girl Who Cares

CHAPTER 7

HAGAR

he Used Girl

Hagar

A 3 Day Study

Before You Start:

Hagar was a slave to Sarah, Abraham's wife in the book of Genesis. God promised Abraham and Sarah that he would give them children and that the descendants of that child would be as numerous as the stars in the sky (Genesis 15:5). But Abraham and Sarah were old, and they got tired of waiting to have a child, so they used Hagar to try to get what God promised them.

DAY 1

Girl Read: Genesis Chapter 16:1-6

Girls Life: I can't relate to being used like Hagar, but maybe you can. When Sarah gave up hope that she would have a baby she decided to use Hagar to try to get what God promised. Hagar was like a square piece Sarah tried to place into a circular puzzle. She'd never fit.

Girls are used for many hurtful things: things like sex, their bodies, their looks, gossip, verbal/emotional/physical abuse, or their character. Being used can chip at a girl's self-esteem. Girls are not meant to be used. We are meant to be loved.

Girl Do: *Know your value.*

We are not the things that have been done to us. We are the girl's God says we are. We are loved (Romans 8:35-39). We are not a mistake (Psalms 139:13-18). We are chosen (Ephesians 1:4-6). And like we will read about Hagar on day 2 of this Hagar study, we are seen by God.

If you are in a situation where you are being used and you need help, I encourage you to reach out to someone close to you. Regardless of what the person who is using you may say, you have great worth. God loves you and other people love you. Find a safe person to talk to.

And to the girls like me who have been blessed not to have been used, be the one to step in and helps those who are. Be the person another girl can talk to. You might not have all the answers, but you can make a difference by listening, encouraging, and helping her find the resources she needs to get help.

Girl Ask: Do I believe that I am the girl God says I am regardless of what has been done to me?

DAY 2

Girl Read: Genesis Chapter 16:7-16

Girls Life: I once sat on a bench and told God that I was done trying to save myself from the anorexia that consumed me and the cutting that I couldn't control.

"If I'm going to live through this then you're going to have to save me," I said.

And you know what? The very next day God reached into my situation and saved me. I couldn't believe that he cared for ME.

Hagar called God El-Roi in the desert which means, 'God sees me.' She was just a pregnant slave girl, but God saw her. He sees you too.

Girl Do: *Live like God sees you and cares for you because he does!*

You might think you're just a high school girl, a college girl, a married girl, a mom, or a used girl. But it doesn't matter what kind of label you put on yourself. God sees you. Talk to

God today and tell him everything you think he doesn't see and all the hurt you carry. You may not get an answer right away, or you may not get an answer at all, but if you read God's word you will see that God is good and he loves even the seemingly insignificant people. He saw Hagar the slave, and Shelbie the anorexic and cutter. He loves us all. He loves YOU.

Girl Ask: Do I think God cares enough about me to see me?

DAY 3

Girl Read: Genesis Chapter 21:1-21

Girl Life: I've lain in the darkness of my bedroom, stared at the shadows on the ceiling, and wondered if God cared about me. Even after God showed me he cared by answering my prayers I still sometimes wonder. But Jesus says that he is with us always (Matthew 28:20). God saw Hagar and Ishmael in the desert, and he saved them a second time. Hagar's story is proof that God sees the used girls, the less-than girls, the shamed girls, the broken girls, and he loves them. He saves them. And that includes you and me.

Girl Do: *Don't doubt God's love for you.*

You are so adored. God loves you more than you can comprehend. If you have one more minute read Isaiah 43:1-4. I know that's a lot of reading for one day, but you need to know how special you are. Live your life like God sees you, loves you, and like you are adored. Because, friend, you are. I doubt God's love and affection sometimes too, but when we have those down days, we can remember that God saw Hagar, the slave girl in the desert, and saved her not once, but *twice*.

Girl Ask: What words or verses from today can I remind myself of when I don't feel like God cares about me?

A LETTER TO THE USED GIRL

Dear Used Girl,

Nothing you have done or that has been done to you is too much for God to heal. God sees the wounds you hide on the outside and inside of your body. He sees the hurt in your heart and the pain in your soul. It's easy to wonder why God would allow these things to happen to you, but I assure you, dear friend, that God's heart has hurt with yours. There has not been one second that he has not been with you, not one painful thing that he is not aware of. He wants to heal your wounds and hug you close.

"If you'll hold on to me for dear life," says God,

"I'll get you out of any trouble.

I'll give you the best of care

if you'll only get to know and trust me.

Call me and I'll answer, be at your side in bad times;

I'll rescue you, then throw you a party.

Psalms 91:14-15 (MSG)

I can't tell you why bad things have happened to you, but I know that God did not cause them to happen. We live in a broken world with broken people. Sometimes those people make choices that hurt God's heart. If someone has used you, reach out to God, El-Roi, the God who sees. El-Roi can handle your pain, anger, and hurt in regard to what has happened. Tell him everything. Let him heal you.

Dear girl, know that you are seen, *really* seen. Hagar was not popular or rich, she was a slave. God saw a slave girl in the desert and saved her twice. Whether you are in a posh house, a car, a treatment center, a trailer, a sorority house, or outside, God can see you. He cares for you as he cared for Hagar.

From,

A Girl Who Cares

CHAPTER 8
ABIGAIL

he Smart Girl

ABIGAIL

A 3 DAY STUDY

BEFORE YOU START:

Abigail was a wife of King David in the Old Testament. But before she was David's wife, she was married to a villainous man named Nabal. Her story of meeting and marrying David takes place after David killed the giant Goliath, but before he was crowned king of Israel. For many years David ran from his predecessor, Saul, who wanted him dead because God wanted David to be king instead of Saul. This story takes place during the years David was on the run.

93

DAY 1

Girl Read: I Samuel Chapter 25:1-19

Girl Life: I've talked to many girls who have had things done or said to them that were wrong. They have been hurt by the people around them. People who were supposed to love them but instead of love, they were met with hurtful words, abuse, or pain. While I could not go back in time and right those wrongs in a palpable way, I could look them in the eyes and tell them that God loves them no matter what.

Abigail thought that Nabal's refusal to help David and his men was wrong. She saw an injustice and did her best to right the wrong of Nabal.

We can't always right wrongs, but sometimes we can. We can donate money to a family who's struggling with hospital bills, speak truth to a friend, or offer time or money to help someone rebuild after a natural disaster. Abigail saw what Nabal did wrong and did all she could to make it right.

Girl Do: *Don't be afraid to make a wrong right.*

Abigail could have sat back in her tent and watched David kill Nabal. Nabal was not a kind man and doing nothing might have benefited her if she no longer wanted to be married to an evil man. Instead of sitting back and letting David kill her husband for refusing to help him she stepped into a heated situation because she knew it was the right thing to do.

Girl Ask: Is there a wrong I can make right?

DAY 2

Girl Read: I Samuel Chapter 25:20-35

Girl Life: There are times in my marriage where I do not speak as wisely or humbly to my husband as Abigail spoke to David. Instead of being soft-spoken, I get frustrated and speak without thinking, knowing my words will hurt Mason's feelings. I doubt many of us act calmly in heated situations which is one of the reasons Abigail is such a wonderful role model. David was *angry*. Angry enough to kill not only Abigail's husband but every male in his household. Abigail reasoned with David, she told him that God was the one who avenged David in the past. She reminded David that he didn't need to overreact because God had a plan for David's life.

Girl Do: *Speak with God's wisdom and respect.*

One of the first things Abigail did was kneel in front of David, recognizing him as the man God had chosen to be king over Israel. She took the guilt of her husband on herself and gave David the food he asked for in the first place. Her soft-spoken wisdom cooled David's anger and halted him in his tracks. Let this be a reminder to us to be calm, wise, and discerning of situations instead of reciprocating anger with anger.

Girl Ask: In what area of my life do I need to respond with wisdom and respect rather than anger?

DAY 3

Girl Read: I Samuel Chapter 25:36-42

Girl Life: I wonder where God is when I read news stories about the terrible things being done to people all over the world. Where is God in those situations? Does he see? The answer is, yes. Sometimes God answers injustice right away, and other times we don't see it. In today's reading, we see God enact justice following the events between David, Nabal, and Abigail. It's good to be reminded that God sees and that he is a God of justice.

Girl Do: *Know that God is a God of justice.*

God's judgment on Nabal was swift and final. After the death of her husband, God provided for Abigail by giving her the option of marrying David, the future king of Israel. I think David would have respected Abigail if she chose not to marry him. We know from her previous encounter with David that God could have given her the right words. The way God exercises his judgment, power, and love toward Abigail after she helped David should give us faith that God

99

sees us too. God does not always strike bad people dead or provide for us in such a tangible way as he did for Abigail. But reading his word gives us a peek at who God is. And he is a good God. Filled with justice and love.

Girl Ask: Do I believe that God is a good judge?

A LETTER TO THE
SMART GIRL

Dear Smart Girl,

You are wise and discerning which are excellent qualities to have. Your life is filled with avenues to grow smarter. Higher education and the wisdom of your peers and elders surround you. You have a wealth of articles and facts at your fingertips with the Internet.

But dear, smart, girl, please remember that true wisdom comes from God.

"'The fear of the LORD is the beginning of

wisdom;

all who follow his precepts have good

understanding...'" Psalm 111:10

Living with true smarts means that you search God's word for insight and then act on the truths he shows you. God makes it clear that what most people consider wisdom is not true wisdom.

"'Where is the wise man? Where is the scholar? Where is the philosopher of this age? Has not God made foolish the wisdom of the world?. . . Christ the power of God and the wisdom of God. For the foolishness of God is wiser than man's wisdom, and the weakness of God is stronger than man's strength.'" 1 Corinthians 1:20 & 24-25

You can be considered one of the smartest girls in the room, but if your wisdom is not rooted in God it is not the fullness that it can be.

Abigail was both wise and humble. She righted wrongs with her wisdom. If you want to follow in her footsteps look for ways to delicately and humbly right the wrongs around you. Be quick to look to God for wisdom and not yourself. Trust that God is just and good. Lean into his amazing rightness. Use your smarts to lead people toward God and his truth.

Keep being smart, girl. You are amazing.

From,

A Girl Who Cares

CHAPTER 9

LEAH

The Unloved Girl

Leah

A 3 Day Study

Before You Start:

The story of Leah is closely tied to the story of her sister, Rachel. Through an unfortunate turn of events, they both married the same man. Leah, Rachel, and their maids became the mothers of the twelve tribes of Israel which played an integral role in the rest of the Bible. They were married to Jacob who God later renamed Israel.

DAY 1

Girl Read: Genesis Chapter 29:1-30

Girl Life: At the age of 13, between red lockers and white brick walls, I discovered that I was unwanted. The boys I admired talked about other girls while leaving me out of the conversation. In high school, and for a short time after, I went unnoticed as far as romance. I felt left out and unlovable. Imagine Leah's hurt when she was given in marriage to a man who did not want her. Relating to Leah is easy because we can all think of a time when we felt unwanted.

Girl Do: *Know that you are wanted.*

I can think of no better way to encourage us that we are wanted than to share a few of my favorite verses. While we all want the love of a guy in our life, we can know that regardless of if we are rejected, God loves us always.

Because I am God, your personal God,

The Holy of Israel, your Savior.

I paid a huge price for you:

all of Egypt, with rich Cush and Seba thrown in!

That's how much you mean to me!

That's how much I love you!

I'd sell off the whole world to get you back,

trade the creation just for you.

Isaiah 43: 3-4 (MSG)

Girl Ask: Do I believe that I am wanted by God?

DAY 2

Girl Read: Genesis Chapter 29:31-35

Girl Life: Throughout my years of singleness I never stopped believing in and trusting God. When a guy passed me by, I was deeply hurt but held on to the fact that God loved me. I had faith that someday I'd find a man who loved me, too.

Since Jacob loved Rachel more, Leah had to lean into God's love. She expressed her feelings in the naming of her sons. The name of her first son Reuben acknowledged that God saw her. Her second son, Simeon, that God heard her. The naming of her third son was a plea for her husband to love her and be connected to her. Levi's name means "attached." Then she named her fourth son Judah which means "praise." Each name represented what she was feeling in her life about God and Jacob.

Girl Do: *Praise God when you feel unloved.*

God's love for us does not change regardless of the way we feel or the way we are treated. Leah wasn't loved, but she didn't let that stop her from leaning into God's love and truth. We should learn from her and praise him in the hard times. When we can't see a bright spot in our lives, we should praise God anyway. When we feel unloved, we can be confident that God loves us. Jacob may not have shown great love to Leah in the story, but God did. God gave Leah the most prized possession of a woman in her day and time, sons. Instead of becoming resentful with the birth of each son and no more love from her husband, Leah named her fourth son Judah. Praise to God.

Girl Ask: How does God show me he loves me when I feel unloved by the people around me?

DAY 3

Girl Read: Genesis Chapter 30:1-24

Girl Life: God does not answer all my prayers. There are things I've prayed that I have yet to see come to pass. Yet, I still pray. I pray because I know from experience and from stories like Leah's that God hears me. Verse 17 of today's reading says, *"God listened to Leah."* If God heard Leah, we can be sure that he hears us, too.

Girl Do: *Live like God hears you.*

I have a confession to make . . . I do not pray as much as I should. Maybe I'm lazy, maybe I need to discipline myself more, or maybe, on some level, I wonder if God hears me. I *know* God hears me but *believing* that he hears me is hard. I know God hears me because he has answered my prayers in very tangible ways in the past, but my brain finds it easy to forget. There is a little piece of my heart that wonders why God would listen to a girl like me. Who am I that God would listen when there are girls all around the world praying for much more important things like food, shelter, and safety?

Here are the words from verse 17 again, *"God listened to Leah."* God listened. He hears. If we want to live like God hears us, we need to talk to God more like a best friend rather than an uninterested father figure in the sky. Because the truth is, he does hear. It's you and I who have trouble believing.

Girl Ask: Do I believe that God hears me?

A LETTER TO THE UNLOVED GIRL

Dear Unloved Girl,

Regardless of how you feel, you *are* loved. When you see your friends finding love or getting married and no man is holding your hand it's hard to believe you are loved. But you are. You are loved immeasurably.

"For I am convinced that neither death nor life, neither angels nor demons, neither the present nor the future, nor any powers, neither height nor depth, nor anything else in all creation, will be able to separate us from the love of God that is in Christ Jesus our Lord." Romans 8:38-39

You hear songs about the physical act of love. You attend weddings. You watch movies where two people fall into love seamlessly and unendingly. You are surrounded by love. This is a hard culture to live in when you are single or in a loveless relationship. Your heart has a physical ache that you feel can only be filled with the love of a significant other. Nevertheless, you must not disregard the love you already have.

God's love.

That could come across as lame, but if you consider it, you will find that it is anything but.

When I think of God's love and try to compare it with human love I am met with a feeling of fullness and emptiness. Human love, physical love, is amazing, erotic, and pleasurable. But God's love is full, true, and all-consuming. It fills. I've been tantalized by both kinds of love, but only one makes me feel whole. Physical love has a full feeling at the moment but leaves much to be desired. It does not feed the soul the same way God's love does.

This, dear girl, is why you don't have to walk around feeling unloved because you don't have a boyfriend or you're not married. As a married girl, I must tell you that you already have the most amazing part of love you will ever have. Yes, marriage to a man who loves you is amazing and worthwhile, but it's a representation of true love which is God's love. If you can accept God's love into your life you will know that you are full. He can be what you need.

I know these might not be words you want to hear. You might disregard them based on the fact that I am in a married relationship. I get that. I am not in your shoes. But I know God and if I could go back in time and talk to my sad single self, I would try to convey to her the fullness of God's love. I would tell her that marriage and sex cannot fulfill her. I would hug her, cry with her, and tell her that she is so loved no matter what and that her relationship with God is more powerful than any relationship she could ever have with a man.

And girl, this is what I want to tell you.

God's love is full, powerful, and bigger than married love. You are loved no matter what your relationship status. You are amazing. God *loves* you. Try to understand God's love before you get married so you can bring that love into your relationship and be a representation of true love in your marriage. Ultimately that is what marriage is about, imitating God's love to you by loving your spouse unconditionally.

From,

A Girl Who Cares

CHAPTER 10
THE SHUNAMMITE WOMAN

he Optimistic Girl

The Shunammite Woman

A 3 Day Study

Before You Start:

The Shunammite Women was not given a formal name in Scripture. Her story took place in the Old Testament in the book of 2 Kings between the time of King David and the exile of Israel to Babylon. (Or if that's still confusing: the time between King David near the center of your Bible, and the time of Jesus in the last third of your Bible.) Her story was precluded by another story about a woman whom Elisha also helped.

DAY 1

Girl Read: 2 Kings Chapter 4:8-10

Girl Life: I love entertaining people at my house. We don't do it often, but when we do, I enjoy making fresh cookies and turning on music. If it's a movie night I make popcorn on the stovetop—if I'm honest I make it when there is no movie, too. Fresh gooey chocolate chip cookies and crunchy popcorn are my things. The Shunammite Woman was introduced in Scripture for her hospitality. She and her husband built a second story to their house so they could accommodate Elisha whenever he passed through town. Her generosity and warmth are our first glimpses into her life.

Girl Do: *Offer kindness and hospitality to those God puts in your path.*

If you are in high school or college this could mean welcoming a new student. If you have an apartment or a home this could mean inviting someone over for dinner. If you are married with a child maybe this means inviting your kids' best friend and his/her parents over. If you attend church this could mean introducing yourself to someone who is visiting your church for the first time. Don't only offer hospitality to Christians, welcome all people into your home and life. Jesus primarily hung out with the outcasts. We should be hospitable to people in our social circles and those outside of them.

Girl Ask: Who can I be hospitable to today?

DAY 2

Girl Read: 2 Kings Chapter 4:11-37

Girl Life: Words, images, and pain have been etched into my memories from times when someone I loved died. I don't ever remember saying, "Everything is all right," in those moments. When I've been told through tears that someone I love has passed away, everything is *not* all right. To be honest, things are horrible. But the Shunammite Woman? She said, "Everything is all right." Did she trust that God would raise her son from the dead or did she just love God enough to know that no matter the outcome everything would be all right? I don't know, but when I read about her, I am inspired by her optimism.

Girl Do: *Trust God that everything will be all right.*

If the Shunammite Woman who lost her son could say that everything was all right, then I think we should give it a try. I don't know what you are going through but trust God. Maybe it starts as a whisper of hope in your soul but try it.

Say, "Everything is all right." Because ultimately, if you love God and have accepted his son, everything *is* all right. You are a loved child of God and death does not separate you from that love but draws you closer.

Girl Ask: Do I believe that everything is all right?

DAY 3

Girl Read: 2 Kings Chapter 8:1-6

Girls Life: When I was 15, I left my family and friends and went to live at a place called Mercy Multiplied to find healing from my eating disorder. Before I left, my relationships were strained, but when I returned, God restored them and gave me more life than I had before I left. The Shunammite Woman listened when Elisha told her to leave her home and when she returned, everything she owned was restored to her.

Girl Do: *Leave behind what God asks you to leave and go where he has called you to go.*

I don't know what your life will look like when you come back, but I do know that when God tells me to do something there is life and joy on the other side of saying, "Yes." Trust God with what he asks you to leave behind and follow him. I doubt you'll ever regret it.

Girl Ask: Is there somewhere God wants me to go? Can I trust God with what I leave behind?

A LETTER TO THE
OPTIMISTIC GIRL

Dear Optimistic Girl,

Your faith in life and God is beautiful. You believe the best in people, which is a gift, girl. Not all people can see life through a promising lens.

Life is hard. You already know this. I'm sure you have experienced some pain like the Shunammite Woman. You have walked hard paths, cried many tears, and clung to hope when all seemed hopeless. But girl, everything will be all right.

If you can, now, declare, "Everything *is* all right." Everything may not be all right in our lives now, but we can have faith that God will use even our pain. We must trust that God sees the bigger picture and one day everything *will* be all right.

"'And we know that in all things God works for the good of those who love him, who have been called according to his purpose.'"
Romans 8:28

Girl, cling to that optimism you carry. Don't let the darkness or hard times kill that light in you. Have faith that God has you in the palm of his hand and knows every struggle you are facing.

"'your eyes saw my unformed body.

All the days ordained for me

were written in your book

before one of them came to be.'" Psalms 139:16

God knows every part of your life. He knew them before you were born. He knows the hardships you will face.

The Shunammite Woman had her land restored to her after she left everything behind to obey the words of God's prophet and everything worked out. Things in our lives do not always happen the way we planned or intended. A lot of times we find ourselves in a place we never foresaw. But God is in those places. Many times, God led us to those places.

Girl, God loves you and I believe he loves your optimism. Don't let go of that gift. Share your light with those around you and cling to God when darkness comes.

And remember, "Everything is all right."

From,

A Girl Who Cares

CHAPTER 11

ESTHER

he Brave Girl

ESTHER

A 14 DAY STUDY

BEFORE YOU START:

Not every day in this reading plan is about Esther. This study encompasses the entire 10 chapters of Esther. Don't worry, you can do it! I think it's important to read the whole story to understand who Esther was and how we can learn from her. She doesn't need much preamble since we'll be reading her whole story.

DAY 1

Girl Read: Esther Chapter 1:1-12

Girl Life: I'm in the process of trying to find my next Insta-gramable (is that a word?) photo. I've been on this (not so serious) quest for several days. Last night I flipped my phone out to take a photo of Mason and me in the car but no, who wants to see a picture like that? I'll admit that I like to post photos of myself. I like comments, likes, and views. I like to feel beautiful and validated which makes me wonder, why did Queen Vashti refuse an opportunity to show off?

The king asked her to wear her crown and show off her beauty. Yet she refused.

I see where Queen Vashti's hesitation could have come from. Women in Biblical times didn't have the freedom we have now. Part of Queen Vashti's worth seems to come from her beauty. Maybe like us, she didn't like being only an object of attraction. Maybe she wanted her heart to be known. It's also possible she just wanted to be rude. The Bible doesn't say, so we are left to speculate.

Girl Do: *Find your worth in God, not yourself.*

Maybe we don't look like Queen Vashti or the girl on social media, but we are all beautiful. Each one of us has a trait, a characteristic, that can come only from us. We are girls and we are beautiful, but we should not let ourselves be blinded by even our most beautiful attributes. Looks do not define who we are and neither does our next Instagram picture. The worth and sum of our beauty should come from how much we love God and how we show the world that love.

Girl Ask: Has my beauty (remember, we all are beautiful) ever caused me to make an unpopular decision?

DAY 2

Girl Read: Esther Chapter 1:13-22

Girl Life: I'm glad Mason doesn't kick me out of the house whenever I don't come at his first call as the king did to Queen Vashti. To be honest I'm normally the one calling for him. "Mas, can you bring me a glass of water? Mas, can you come to say goodnight to me? Mas, will you run up the stairs to hug me?"

In our reading today the king issued an order for women to honor their husbands. As girls and women in the twenty-first century, we might find that scary and unfair. Even if we're not married, we might worry that being commanded to submit to our husbands someday might cause us to be abused emotionally, verbally, spiritually, or physically. But I can assure you the idea is quite Biblical and in Biblical context, safe.

Girl Do: *Understand that women are not meant to be dominated by men.*

I think girls get the wrong idea about what God says about honoring our husbands. Some girls may have even heard the word 'submit,' but let's clear this up. If you're not married, you can lock this away for a future day. It's important to know. The passage of Scripture that lines up with the decree of the king in Esther chapter one comes from Ephesians 5:22-33. But sometimes we read the 'submit' part and miss the rest,

"...husbands ought to love their wives as their own bodies. He who loves his wife loves himself." Ephesians 5:28

Girls are not called to be pushed around by men, but rather, to share mutual respect and relationship with God and with their husbands. This is an act of respect from both parties. The man respects God and loves his wife as Christ loves us, unconditionally. If a man loves us as God loves us, then we won't be able but to love him back.

Girl Ask: How do I feel about women submitting to their husbands?

DAY 3

Girl Read: Esther Chapter 2:1-20

Girl Life: I'm apprehensive to share these private words with you because I don't want to make myself sound conceited, but I think they demonstrate what Esther was to the people around her. When I packed my bags to make the move from Michigan to Florida, I received many notes but these two I have kept and treasured. Here are brief experts from both:

"I've never really known anyone like you who has such a sincere, grateful approach to life. I feel like I have gained so much and learned so much from spending time with you."

Another girl wrote,

"Thanks for being a friend, for your understanding & willingness to reach out. I've only known you a short while, but the spark I see in you sets my heart on fire with love and acceptance of myself."

I could be completely myself with the girls who wrote these notes and was not actively *trying* to make a difference in their lives. We were true friends. I'm not trying to make myself sound cool or brag on myself, but you need to know that your influence is impacting people around you in ways you don't know. I didn't know these girls felt this way until they handed me these handwritten letters. The way you love God shines through your life like pinpricks of hopeful stars in a dark world.

Girl Do: *Go shine in dark places.*

Esther not only found favor with the king but also with all of those around her. Like being a Christian in a mainstream world, Esther was a Jew in a non-Jewish world. The light of God in her shined through. You are the same. God is a light in you.

Girl Ask: How can I grow closer to God so that people see him in me?

DAY 4

Girl Read: Esther Chapter 2:21-23

Girl Life: It's easy to ignore the things around us, shrug our shoulders, and say, "I'm sure someone else will take care of it." I've done this before. I've seen homeless people holding signs and have thought; *Someone else will give them money.* My chest aches in these moments because I know I should do something, or I can't and wish I could. We're comfortable with looking the other way, not getting involved, or reasoning our way out of the callings God places on our hearts. Maybe we see someone being bullied, ignore the girl with a haunted look in her eyes, or close our eyes to the pain and injustice around us.

Girl Do: *Act in your circle of influence.*

Esther's cousin Mordecai heard about a plot to kill the king and did something about it. He acted and his action saved the life of the king. We need to act in our circles of influence. We should be wise and get someone more experienced involved if we don't know what to do or are dealing with a serious situation. But we need to open our eyes and ears to see those around us who need us. Maybe we need to sit by someone who is alone, maybe we need to tell our Moms we love them, maybe we need to let our little sister spill her heart out to us or maybe we need to encourage a friend who's going through a hard time. Let's let God guide us to be open to the needs of those around us.

Girl Ask: Have I been shutting myself off to helping people because I'm more comfortable not getting involved?

DAY 5

Girl Read: Esther Chapter 3:1-6

Girl Life: Have you ever gone along with what everyone else is doing so you don't stand out even if you don't agree with what is being done or said? I've stood in circles and laughed at jokes I didn't find funny because I didn't want to go against the flow. My Christian beliefs are not always the popular belief and I've found myself following the crowd. Mordecai disobeyed a royal command to bow to Haman and in the process stuck out from the crowd. I think Mordecai's refusal to bow to Haman had to do with his belief in God and his obedience to God's laws. Bowing can be like worship and God told the Jewish people, *"You shall have no other gods before me."* Exodus 20:3

Girl Do: *Don't compromise.*

Compromising what we believe to fit in will leave us feeling guilty and icky inside. If we love God, we need to be brave and stand up for what we believe. Maybe this means not going to a certain party, hanging out with a friend who you know will tempt you to disrespect God or saying something you don't agree with to receive approval. Whatever it is, we should let God's Spirit guide us to do what is right and not compromise on our beliefs.

Girl Ask: Have I ever done something I regretted or doesn't align with what I believe to win the approval of others?

DAY 6

Girl Read: Esther Chapter 3:7-15

Girl Life: We all know about World War II and the Jewish Holocaust, but did you know there was almost a Jewish Holocaust in Bible times too? There is very real evil in our world. I don't understand men like Haman or Hitler who wanted a whole people group killed. The only things I want to die in its entirety are cockroaches and spiders. Seriously, I scream when I see cockroaches. God chose the Jewish people to be his own. If we believe in God, then we also must believe in the devil. It stands to reason that evil would want to kill the thing that God loves.

Girl Do: *Shine a light on the hatred in your heart.*

We're quick to point fingers and tell the people around us that they are single-minded, hurtful, and wrong, but how often do we recognize the hatred in our hearts? Haman took his hatred to the extreme, but we should be aware of it in our own lives too. We should respond to those we dislike with the same love Jesus demonstrated to all people. Let's not repeat history and let's shine a light on the dark parts of our hearts.

Girl Ask: Can I identify any hatred in my heart that I need to give to God?

DAY 7

Girl Read: Esther Chapter 4:1-17

Girl Life: I walked the halls of the residential facility that housed forty girls. My six months were almost up, and I was about to return to home and high school with knowledge and tools to help me live in freedom from my eating disorder, self-harm, and depression. Although I was still healing, I felt this pull, an irresistible tug on my heart. I knew in my soul that God wanted me to help girls struggling with eating disorders and body image issues and I knew it involved writing. So, at sixteen I began my writing journey because it was what God wanted me to do. We all have certain things God has placed on our hearts, things we were created to do. Some of them are obvious like being a big sister, a mother, or a good friend, but other things are whispered to our hearts.

Girl Do: *Do what God has called you to do.*

Do you know that thing in your heart that you can't stop thinking about? That passion? You were born right here, in this place, with this influence, because God wants to use you and your gifts. Maybe you are a student, painter, encourager, dancer, teacher, counselor, scientist, or mother. No matter what it is, God made you for that thing. Esther had a purpose, a reason she became queen, a calling. She was called to speak on behalf of a nation under the threat of certain death. It was scary, but she chose to do it because it was God's task for her.

Girl Ask: What has God placed on my heart for me to do?

DAY 8

Girl Read: Esther Chapter 5:1-14

Girl Life: Excitement and fear warred within me as I drove my little silver Honda-CRV with my dog in the passenger seat and all my belongings packed in the back over the state line and into Florida. I left behind the home I'd had my whole life, my friends, my job, my family, and what was familiar to risk moving. My risk was small in comparison to Esther's. I risked disliking my new home and wishing for what was behind while she risked her life. We all risk things. We risk friendships for the sake of honesty, loss of familiarity when we choose a college, and move out of our bedrooms, our hearts when we chose to date or marry. Risk is a part of life, but Esther's destiny was located inside risk.

Girl Do: *Take the risk God calls you to.*

Being a risk-taker can be a good or a bad thing depending on the circumstance. Some might have considered Esther's risk a bad thing considering she risked her very life to seek a conversation with the king. But when we look at the other side of her decision, we see that she was risking her one life on behalf of an entire nation of lives. God may ask us to risk something in this adventure called life and we need to be brave enough to take the risk. We should not live in fear of what the risk will cost us, but in expectation of what God can do with us and for us if we trust him.

Girl Ask: Is God asking me to take a risk?

DAY 9

Girl Read: Esther Chapter 6:1-13

Girl Life: I read that another girl achieved the success I strove for by landing an agent or signing a book deal and my heart sank. Ugly things rose out of the hurt in my heart: *Why does she get that instead of me? I've worked just as hard. I'm better than her. How did this happen?* I knew this thinking wasn't right. I knew I was in the wrong for my bitter thoughts. I had to change my perspective and remember that we are all in this together! We girls are not enemies striving for the last brownie, (or a book deal, college degree, job, baby, husband or house) we're sisters working in the same kitchen. We don't need to rush to get the last piece of something. We need to work together and help one another. If we read Esther chapter 6, we know that bitterness is not a good look on anyone. We should not feel bitter or angry because of another's success. We should cheer them on!

Girl Do: *Elevate others above yourself in a stance of grace and love.*

Haman had to elevate Mordecai after a botched attempt to gain his renown backfired. We should elevate others above ourselves instead of trying to be the one in the spotlight. We are just human, and as such, we need to help our fellow humans out. God is the one who deserves the ultimate praise. We should love others as he loves us, unconditionally. We are not meant to run another person's journey. We are meant to run the one God has placed before us and it will look different than the girl in the next lane.

Girl Ask: Is there someone I should be elevating instead of harboring jealousy or bitterness towards?

DAY 10

Girl Read: Esther Chapter 7:1-10

Girl Life: When I'm going through a difficult time one of the hardest things for me to do is ask for help. I don't like admitting I am weak or that I can't figure out life on my own. Esther asked for the ultimate help in saving her people. Some of the things I have asked for help in the past are help fighting my eating disorder, help with the decision of who I should marry, help with my struggles with mental health, or help with something as simple as cleaning the house.

Girl Do: *Ask for help when you need it.*

We all need help sometimes. Maybe, like Esther, after we take a risk, we need to ask for help. Esther asked the king for help and maybe the first person we need to ask for help in our lives is our King, Jesus. After bringing our difficulty to God maybe we need to ask for help from a parent, friend, counselor, teacher, or coworker. Asking for help is not a weakness, it's a sign of strength. We cannot do life on our own. God wants us to talk to him. He wants us to ask him for help, too.

Girl Ask: Is there something I need to ask for help with today?

DAY 11

Girl Read: Esther Chapter 8:1-16

Girl Life: My social media and website are both filled with inspiration for girls to accept, admire, and love the bodies they have been given. This is the thing God has placed on my heart to speak up about. I've seen social media accounts where girls voice their passion to end human trafficking, eliminate distorted eating, encourage finding the right kind of love, and how to cultivate healthy relationships. Each of the women behind these accounts has a passion, something they know they cannot stay silent about. Esther didn't stay silent about her people. She was the voice of a nation, a voice of hope, a voice of life.

Girl Do: *You have a voice! Speak up!*

We want to hear from you. God has given you something to say. We all have different passions. What is the thing you can't keep inside of you anymore? Are you passionate about the homeless, the bullied, the starving, the silenced, the abused, the empty? Consider this a nudge to accept that stirring in your soul to help those people and go out there and speak up. This doesn't mean you have to be an influencer on social media or do radio interviews. No, this means speaking up where God places you and that might be as narrow as your home and friend group or as wide as international recognition. Follow where he leads and be obedient to the stirrings of God in your heart.

Girl Ask: What do I need to speak up about?

DAY 12

Girl Read: Esther Chapter 9:1-19

Girl Life: You know that scene in *Beauty and the Beast* where the teapot, the clock, the candelabra, the stool, the wardrobe, and all the other inhabitants of the castle hide in the shadows and then defend their home against the intruders? I don't know exactly why, but this story in the Bible reminds me of that. I know it sounds silly. This is a G-rated example of what happened in today's passage.

The Jews defended themselves. Some people wanted to hurt and kill them, and they defended their homes, families, lives, and possessions from destruction. I doubt any of us need to defend ourselves from death but maybe we need to defend ourselves from verbal, physical, or emotional abuse. Maybe we need to defend someone who can't defend themselves.

Girl Do: *Don't be afraid to defend yourself or another.*

I don't recommend being violent, but I do think we should defend ourselves. This could look like standing up to somebody, defending your beliefs to someone who talks down about you, God, or your faith. This could be defending the less fortunate by getting involved in a program to help them or speaking up as we talked about on Day 11 of our Esther study. Like the Jews, we are children of God, we are part of his family. Being a child of God does not mean we are weak. It means we are his and he is our strength.

Girl Ask: Do I need to defend myself or someone else today?

DAY 13

Girl Read: Esther Chapter 9:20-32

Girl Life: Did you know that the holiday of Purim is still celebrated today? I am blessed to have married into a beautiful family who celebrates Jewish holidays and Purim is one of them. Purim is a celebration of God's faithfulness to his people. God rescued an entire nation from destruction, and he used Esther to accomplish that. This is a testament to the fact that God can use us, even girls, to do BIG things.

Girl Do: *Celebrate God's faithfulness in your life.*

What has God done for you recently? Maybe he brought a new friend into your life, helped you through a hard day, or maybe you need to thank him for being faithful and never leaving you. Whatever it is, celebrate it. Tell a friend or family member, give a gift to someone, make an awesome meal to share, spend some time in prayer, tell God you are thankful. Celebrate!

Girl Ask: What has God done for me recently that I can celebrate?

DAY 14

Girl Read: Esther Chapter 10:1-3

Girl Life: The book of Esther closes with an account of Mordecai, the father figure to Esther. Neither Mordecai nor Esther would have accomplished all they did if they hadn't been obedient to God's call to risk everything to save the Jewish people. It may seem like it was Esther who took the risk, but Mordecai asked his family, his adopted daughter, to do something only she could do at the risk of losing her life. Mordecai loved Esther and Esther loved her people. The book of Esther teaches us that there are things in our lives only we can do and that we might have to take risks to accomplish them.

Girl Do: *Don't push away the call of God on your life because it's scary.*

I don't know how the risks I take or the risks you take will turn out. There are many different examples and outcomes in history, but we learn from Esther and Mordecai that taking a risk can place us exactly where God wants us. If we are hesitant or scared, we should ask for help, like Esther, and follow God no matter what.

Girl Ask: What does God want me to do that only I can do?

A LETTER TO THE
BRAVE GIRL

Dear Brave Girl,

Your bravery and willingness to take risks for God is a beautiful attribute that I believe God has placed in you. When you fear, turn to God and let him give peace to your heart. Never forget that you are a child of God and that he goes before you.

I look behind me and you're there,

then up ahead and you're there, too—

your reassuring presence, coming and going, Psalms 139:5 (MSG)

Remember that you are never alone. God is always with you in your bravest moments and your weakest moments. Read God's word, ask for help, and follow his call on your heart to take the risk and be brave the way that he wants you to be. Your bravery is beautiful.

Could it be you are NOT brave, but you WANT to be? I believe that you can be. God has placed strength inside each of us and with his help, we can accomplish even the scary things he asks us to do. You are not alone if you are scared sometimes or maybe don't consider yourself brave. I'm scared sometimes, too. I think we all are, but God is bigger and greater than our fears. Let's seek God and be brave together!

From,

A Girl Who Cares

CHAPTER 12

MARY MAGDALENE

he Following Girl

MARY MAGDALENE

A 3 DAY STUDY

BEFORE YOU START:

Mary Magdalene is mentioned in all four of The Gospels. (The books of Matthew, Mark, Luke, and John in the New Testament) She was a follower of Jesus throughout his ministry and was also present for his death and resurrection. There has been speculation whether the sinful woman who anoints Jesus' feet in Luke 7:36-50 could be Mary Magdalene. Since her name is not mentioned explicitly in the text this study will not include those verses. But Luke 7:36-50 is a wonderful story about a woman in scripture, so put it on your list of things to read once you are done with this study. Maybe you can find your own similarities between the sinful woman and yourself through her story.

DAY 1

Girl Read: Luke Chapter 8:1-3 & John 19:25

Girl Life: There are several famous/influential people I like to follow on social media. People that, when they post, I read the caption and double-tap almost every time. Do you have a few of those people, too? Following today looks a lot different than it did even fifteen years ago. When I was in high school, Facebook was fairly new, and if you wanted the latest news about someone famous you had to find it in a magazine or article. Lives were not lived with pretty captions and hashtags.

Girl Do: *Follow Jesus.*

If following was different fifteen years ago, imagine what it was like *thousands* of years ago. Mary Magdalene was a follower of Jesus. This meant that she literally strapped on her sandals every day and followed him down the dusty road. Her type of following takes the word to a whole new level (or old level if you think about it). She followed Jesus from town to town, to the cross, and his gravesite. Following

Jesus today also looks different from what Mary did or what we do on social media. Although, it would be nice if Jesus had an Instagram account we could follow. Can I get an amen? What following Jesus today looks like is being obedient. We follow him by trusting, believing, and living a life that pleases him. We follow him by loving God first and people second.

Girl Ask: How do I follow Jesus?

DAY 2

Girl Read: John Chapter 20:1-16

Girl Life: I woke up the day after my boyfriend (who later became my husband) broke up with me with a desperate need to find Jesus. The days following our first breakup (yes there were more than one) were filled with Bible reading, listening to Christian music, and desperate talks with God. I knew only God could heal the hurt in my heart and make things right. So, I searched and clung to him wherever I could find his presence. I looked for his voice in the pages of the Bible, the music I listened to, the sermons I attended, and the places in-between. Sometimes I got my desires, or the lies of the enemy confused with God's words and his truth. Sometimes it was hard to recognize him.

Girl Do: *Find Jesus.*

Mary was so broken after the death of Jesus that she didn't recognize him when she saw him after his resurrection. He may have looked different, but I think it was her hurt and belief in his death that kept her eyes from being able to see him clearly. We have the same problem today. We don't always recognize Jesus when we see him. Jesus doesn't always look like a bible verse or a prophecy. Sometimes Jesus looks like a gardener, or maybe in our lives, he could look like a friend, a sunset, or a beautiful display of love. God is everywhere, we must look and be willing to see him in unlikely places.

Girl Ask: Where do you look for Jesus and where have you found him before?

DAY 3

Girl Read: John Chapter 20:17-18

Girl Life: Blank pages in a journal and blinking cursors on the computer screen excite me. Writing is my way of exploring the world God has placed me in and a way for me to share stories or thoughts about him. This book, for example, is a way for me to share what I know about God with you. Four ways I tell people about Jesus are:

1. I write.

2. I talk about him with my friends or small groups.

3. I tell the story of how he saved me.

4. I live my life in a way I hope brings others to wonder who he is and seek him for themselves.

Sharing Jesus can look different for each of us. He gives us different gifts.

Girl Do: *Talk about Jesus.*

We all have different ways of communicating. Some of us are speakers, others are writers, others might be singers, and still, others might communicate with their love. The important thing to do is to get out there and share God's love with the world. Sitting at home watching Netflix and chilling are not going to spread the love of God. There is nothing wrong with nights of Netflix and chill, but we should be doing more than that. Like Mary, we have this joy and hope inside of us we should want to share.

Girl Ask: How do I share Jesus?

A LETTER TO THE
FOLLOWING GIRL

Dear Following Girl,

Have you ever stopped and considered who you follow?
Who is on your top five list? Does God make that list?

Girl, you must be careful who you follow. Following people
is okay if the place they are leading you is closer to God.
There will be some people in life you follow who don't bring
you anywhere bad, but they don't bring you anywhere good
either. It is between you and God whether those are good
people to follow. Here are some questions to ask yourself
when you want to follow someone.

1. Why do I want to follow this person?

2. How does following this person benefit my life?

3. Where will this person ultimately lead me? (Your desires,
satisfaction, your mental health.)

Now, if you ask these same questions about God you will
find these answers.

1. I want to follow God because he saved my life. He loves me more than anyone ever could. He has my best interest in mind. He created me. And my life will be better with him.

2. Following God will benefit me by helping me see the world, people, and his creation through his eyes. I will want to love people and I will see the good things God has placed in them rather than the bad things they let seep out.

3. Following God will lead me into everlasting life with God. As in, I will be able to walk with God as Adam and Eve walked in the garden with God. Following God will lead me to a place where I no longer must be separated from him and I will be able to live with the One who created me and knows me for eternity.

Girl, there is nothing wrong with following people. I follow people for whom I am just curious about their life, but I will challenge myself to reevaluate why I am following them. You are not alone in this. Ask God to give you direction in this area. He will guide you regarding who you should follow and who maybe you should *un*-follow.

Learn from Mary Magdalene. Follow Jesus first and foremost. Then tell those around you how following him as changed your life.

From,

A Girl Who Cares

MORE . . .

BONUS devotional, *The Girl in the Mirror* HERE.

Connect with Shelbie Mae

Instagram (@shelbiemaewrites)

Website (shelbie-mae.com)

Continue to learn more about Shelbie Mae and get a sample of her free *The Girl in the Mirror* devotional . . .

THE GIRL BEHIND THE WORDS

Hey, Girl!

My name is Shelbie and I am the girl behind the words in this book. I am so thankful that you took the time to read these God-inspired words. Writing this book has challenged me and I hope reading it challenged you too.

So, who *AM I*, exactly? Who did you just spend your time with?

As you know, my name is Shelbie Mae. I am an east coast girl currently living on the west coast. I am a twenty-something, married, and also the momma to a cute (but mostly blind) Boston Terrier named Winston who we affectionately call Weenie.

I love reading, running, baking chocolate chip cookies, eating chocolate chip cookies, writing, watching TV, exploring, swimming, hanging out with family and friends, and meeting new people.

What made me want to write a devotional, you may ask? What life experience has led me to this place?

I have a passion for writing to girls because my life was great until it wasn't . . . here's a peek behind the curtain of my life.

I accepted Jesus as my Lord and Savior between the ages of 5 and 8 and spent my first six years of schooling at a private

Christian school. I grew up on the banks of Lake Michigan and lived with my parents who have always loved me and my two sisters—who have *almost* always loved me. If you have siblings, you know what I mean.

I know, my life sounds like a fairy tale, but things took a nasty turn in middle school when I started to doubt God's love for me. This doubt, along with issues in my earthly body, caused me to develop anorexia, which I mentioned in several places in this book.

At the age of 16, I went to a residential program called Mercy Multiplied. At this faith-based program, I was reintroduced to the amazing love of God and I learned to turn the doubts I believed in middle school, around. I realized that God had not abandoned me as I starved my body or dabbled in self-harm. He had been there in every dark bedroom and every sharp object filled bathroom. He loved me more than I could imagine.

But this acceptance of God as a teen and not an elementary student was only a stepping stone on a journey I am continuing to take. Over the years I have dealt with mental health, crippling fear, and depression. But I've also had seasons of strength, courage, fearlessness, and trust. These are the ebbs and flows of my life.

I've been reading my Bible for years. When I discovered that some of the girls I mentored through student ministry at church didn't know Bible stories about girls I wanted to use the knowledge I learned from my days at the Christian school, Mercy Multiplied, my own studies, books read, conversations, and group studies to create a recourse to help these girls dig into the Bible.

This has been incredibly rewarding already. I gave a few chapters of *Girls Like Me* to my sisters. My youngest sister—although she had a similar upbringing—had not heard of some of these women. That, my friend, is why I wrote this book. For you! And I didn't realize it at the time, but I also wrote it for me, because, girl, I have been challenged and touched as well by the things God encouraged me to write.

So, what else do I write?

I have a blog where I encourage girls to live loved, live their purpose, and love their bodies. I also use Instagram to share pieces of my life and encouragement. Sometimes I don't feel like I'm the best example a girl could be because I still struggle in life. But I think that's the point. We will never be perfect apart from Jesus so why not share that journey? There are highs and lows and I try to be real.

Thank you again for taking the time to read this book!

I welcome you followed me on;

Instagram @shelbiemaewrites,

or you can go to my website, shelbie-mae.com.

Remember, girl, you are an amazing and beautiful creation of God. I know that sounds cliché and cheesy, but it is so true. I like to think about God as an artist and me, (us) his art.

You are art, girl.

Yes, YOU!

Love,

Shelbie

Ps. Scroll to the next page to check out the first and second day of a six day study called *The Girl in the Mirror*, a free bonus study on my website to help you see the girl who stares back at you from the mirror the same way God sees her. Because, girl, if you're seeing anything less than beautiful you're not doing it right.

BONUS CONTENT
THE GIRL IN THE MIRROR DEVOTIONAL

Day 1 & 2 of The Girl in the Mirror is included in the following pages. You can download the rest of the devotional at shelbie-mae.com.

THE GIRL IN THE MIRROR
DAY 1

Day 1 - I am Created

Read: Genesis 1:26-28, Psalms 139:13-18 & Ephesians 2:10

How We See Ourselves:

During my tumultuous middle school years where boys crushed on girls from afar to the beat of slamming metal locker doors, I thought, *why did God make some girls beautiful but instead make me ugly?* I knew that God created me, but I thought he made me wrong or didn't put as much thought into me as he did other girls. Why did some girls get to be thin and attractive, but I had the body of a solid athlete?

The first definition of 'create' on Dictonary.com says this: *to cause to come into being, as something unique that would not naturally evolve or that is not made by ordinary processes.*

The very definition of the word create suggests that deep thought went into the process of making the thing in question. For example, I love creating a homey environment in my house. I like my decor to match my style but also make others feel welcome and at ease. Because of my desire to create something beautiful I will sometimes leave walls empty for months while I ponder exactly what I want to go where. When it's done, I stand back and enjoy the finished product, proud of myself for what I've accomplished.

How God Sees Us:

Creating something takes heart, time and thought. With what I know and believe about God now, I believe he made me to look and be exactly who he wanted. I think even my flaws have been carefully considered to bring him glory. My weaknesses are not mistakes. Instead, they are places in life he's given me where I must trust him more, choose him, and believe that there is a purpose for everything.

I don't believe that any of us paints a picture, choreographs a dance, bakes a cake, engineers something grand or fashions something new with halfhearted execution. Many of us will scrap the thing we started making if it doesn't turn out and start again from scratch.

But guess what? If you are reading this, it means you have been created. You are something God thought up and decided he wanted to make. You are valuable to him. He made you the way that you are, the way that you look, and the way you do life. He made YOU. And if God made you then you are good. God called all his creations good. You are not a mistake. The parts of your body you don't like are not mistakes, they are what make you unique. They are what makes you, YOU. And God created, thought out, pondered, visualized, and then artfully created you.

Truth Challenge:

Consider the parts of you that you see as flaws or weaknesses and ponder why God may have given you those things. Look deeper and ask him why he made you with that quirk or curve and look at yourself through the same lens he does. Look at yourself as a girl created by the same God who created your favorite sunset, the blue-green sea, cute puppies, and cocoa beans (Because those are an awesome creation!). What do you see when you look through God's eyes?

Mirror Declaration:

Go stand in front of the mirror and say, "I am created."

THE GIRL IN THE MIRROR
DAY 2

Day 2 - I am Wanted

Read: Genesis 3:8, Exodus 29:45-46 & John 3:16

How We See Ourselves:

There was this boy...(Have you leaned in, yet? I love a good love story.) but he didn't have the same feeling for me as I had for him. I pulled him aside after crushing on him for—I'm a little hesitant to say this—years. Yes, years. I told him how I felt, and he was so sweet and kind as he told me he didn't feel the same way. Yep, that happened.

Then, being the girl I am, I set my sights on another guy but he turned out to be completely oblivious to my interest.

There were some years where I felt unwanted. I didn't have a Valentine's date or any date at any time. No boys were asking for my number. I'd never been kissed, and it seemed like everyone around me had a boyfriend or girlfriend. Can you relate?

I thought having a diamond ring on my finger would ensure I always felt wanted and that I would no longer feel an aching emptiness inside my heart. We girls look for a remedy to this need in many places. We look to guys, jobs, achievements, friends, or our appearance. We desperately want to be wanted. But while the ring I now wear on my finger ensures that my husband has chosen me and wants me as his wife, his love does not fulfill the ache in me. That same yearning desire to be wanted still creeps into my soul.

How God Sees Us:

I imagine God watching us as we struggle and strive to ease the unwanted feelings inside of us. I see him shaking his head in sadness and longing because he knows he can fill that place in our hearts but he's the last place we look. God didn't need to create us. He's God. But why do we create things? It's because we want them. We want the thing we create. It fulfills a purpose or brings us joy. We were created for both of those things. To fulfill the purpose of caring for the earth and the things and people in it and being in a relationship with God.

I love a simple verse tucked into Exodus,

"Then I will dwell among the Israelites and be their God. They will know that I am the LORD their God, who brought them out of Egypt, so that I might dwell among them. I am the LORD their God." Exodus 29:45-46

God could have been content to stay high in the sky, far away from his people, but instead, he wanted to live among them, he wanted them close. He wanted THEM. Their trust, hearts, lives, and love.

In Genesis, after Adam and Eve eat the fruit, we are told that God called out to them while walking in the garden. (Genesis 3:8) God was looking for them. He wanted to be near. He wanted THEM.

One of the most well-known verses in the Bible, John 3:16, tells us that God loved us enough to send his son. He didn't want us to live in sin anymore and made a way for us to live in peace with him.

Repeatedly in scripture, we are reminded that God wants us. He didn't make us and then leave us to muddy up our lives. He created us and then stepped into the brokenness beside us because he wanted to be near. He WANTS us. We are wanted.

It's not easy to live like I'm wanted by God when he seems so far away and the guy I had a crush on (or am married to) is right beside me. I'll admit it's easier to look for the love I can feel with my arms and my lips, but I've also found that it doesn't satisfy me the way that God's love, God's wanting does. I'm not perfect as this, I'm not even great at it, but I'm trying to love God more than anything else. Because when he is near, when I let myself accept that he wants and loves me, something inside becomes whole.

Truth Challenge:

Think about a time when you've felt unwanted. Consider the way God has chosen you and pursued you. Look into those broken moments and see if you can find God.

Mirror Declaration:

Go stand in front of the mirror and say, "I am wanted."

FREE BONUS CHAPTER DOWNLOAD

Download the rest of The Girl in the Mirror devotional at shelbie-mae.com.

ALSO BY SHELBIE MAE

The Kaleidoscope Girl

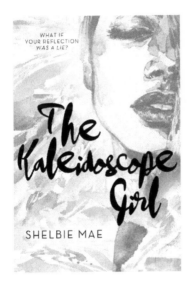

What if your reflection was a lie?

Fresh out of treatment for her eating disorder, seventeen-year-old Ariel uses her journal to recount the perilous days before Hurricane Irma made landfall in Florida. The days she writes about are fragmented images of her past, like the beads at the bottom of a kaleidoscope that make a colorful picture--or a dizzying nightmare. As Ariel recalls those days, her eating disorder causes her to teeter on the edge of recovery and relapse . . . and she's unsure of which side she'd like to fall.

Purchase on Amazon today!

ABOUT THE AUTHOR

Shelbie Mae lives between Michigan, Florida, California, and Oregon with her husband and mostly blind Boston Terrier. She loves baking fresh chocolate chip cookies, running, reading, exploring new places, meeting new friends, and, of course, chilling on the couch with a bowl of popcorn and a movie. You can connect with Shelbie on Instagram, Facebook, Pinterest, or on her Website shelbie-mae.com.

Made in the USA
Columbia, SC
26 August 2021

43771480R00121